Table Of Contents

Preface   5

   Introduction To The Topic   7

   Personal Motivation For Writing The Book   9

   Overview Of The Content   10

Chapter 1: Understanding Clickbait   13

   Definition And Evolution Of Clickbait   43

   The Psychology Of Attention In The Digital Age   44

   Distinction Between Clickbait And Traditional Headlines   47

Chapter 2: The History Of Clickbait   50

   Early Examples In Print And Broadcast Media   52

   Transition To Digital Media   54

   Key Milestones In The Evolution Of Online Clickbait   56

Chapter 3: The Mechanics Of Clickbait   59

   Analysis Of Common Clickbait Strategies   61

   The Role Of Headlines And Visuals   64

   Case Studies Of Successful Clickbait Campaigns   65

Chapter 4: Consumer Psychology   **69**

    Understanding The Psychological Triggers   **71**

    Behavioral Economics Perspectives   **73**

    The Impact Of Clickbait On Reader Emotions And Actions   **75**

Chapter 5: Clickbait In The Age Of Social Media   **78**

    The Role Of Social Media Platforms In Propagating Clickbait   **80**

    How Algorithms Favor Clickbait Content   **82**

    The Social Dynamics Of Sharing Clickbait   **84**

Chapter 6: The Impact On Journalism And Media   **86**

    Effects On Journalistic Standards And Ethics   **88**

    The Balance Between Traffic And Credibility   **90**

    The Economic Incentives Behind Clickbait   **92**

Chapter 7: Ethical And Legal Considerations   **95**

    The Line Between Marketing And Misinformation   **97**

    Legal Cases And Controversies Involving Clickbait   **99**

    Ethical Dilemmas For Content Creators   **101**

Chapter 8: Fighting Back Against Clickbait   **104**

    Tools And Techniques For Identifying Clickbait   **106**

Role Of Media Literacy In Combating Clickbait   108

Initiatives By Platforms And Governments   110

Chapter 9: The Future Of Clickbait   114

Emerging Trends And Technologies   116

Predictions For The Evolution Of Clickbait   118

Potential Impact Of Regulatory Changes   121

Chapter 10: Beyond Clickbait   124

Alternative Strategies For Engagement   126

Success Stories Of Quality Content Over Clickbait   129

The Future Of Responsible Content Creation   132

Conclusion   134

Summarizing The Key Findings And Insights   135

Personal Reflections On The Study Of Clickbait   137

Shaping a Responsible Digital Future   139

Appendix   141

Preface

In an era where the average human attention span competes with the flickering of a screen, and where information is consumed more rapidly than ever before, the phenomenon of clickbait stands as a testament to the evolving landscape of digital media. "A Study of ClickBait" is not just a book; it's an expedition into the heart of this modern digital conundrum, exploring the fine line between captivating content and misleading sensationalism.

My journey into writing this book was sparked by a simple yet persistent question: What makes us click? As a media enthusiast and a consumer of online content, I found myself increasingly fascinated—and at times, frustrated—by the ubiquitous presence of clickbait. This curiosity led me down a path of exploration, seeking to understand not just the mechanics of clickbait, but its implications on information consumption, media ethics, and the psychological underpinnings that make us susceptible to that alluring 'click'.

"A Study of ClickBait" delves into the historical roots of sensationalist content, tracing its evolution from the bold headlines of tabloid newspapers to the sophisticated digital strategies of today's online platforms. Each chapter peels back a layer of this complex phenomenon, examining the intricate dance between consumer psychology, media economics, and technological advancements.

As we navigate through the chapters, we will dissect the anatomy of clickbait, understand its impact on journalism, and confront the ethical dilemmas it presents. We will also explore the role of social media in amplifying clickbait content, and how algorithms and user behavior create a self-perpetuating cycle of sensationalism. Importantly, the book does not just critique; it seeks solutions and strategies for readers, content creators, and platforms to foster a more responsible digital ecosystem.

This book is intended for a diverse audience: from casual readers intrigued by the workings of digital media to professionals and academics seeking a deeper understanding of this phenomenon. It's a synthesis of research, interviews, and case studies, presenting a multifaceted view of clickbait in an accessible and engaging manner.

As you turn these pages, I invite you to not only absorb the information presented but to critically engage with it. "A Study of ClickBait" is more than a study; it's a conversation about the future of our digital landscape and our role in shaping it.

Welcome to the journey. Let's start exploring what really lies behind the click.

Introduction To The Topic

In the ever-evolving landscape of digital media, the term 'clickbait' has emerged as a ubiquitous, yet often misunderstood, phenomenon. At its core, clickbait represents a style of sensationalist content designed to attract attention and encourage visitors to click on a link to a particular web page. However, this simple definition barely scratches the surface of the complex, multifaceted nature of clickbait and its profound impact on how we consume information in the digital age.

This book, "Study of ClickBait," aims to peel back the layers of this phenomenon, offering a comprehensive exploration into not only what clickbait is, but also why it exists, how it works, and what it means for the future of information and media consumption. The journey into the world of clickbait is not just about understanding a marketing tactic; it's about delving into the psychological, sociological, and technological aspects that make clickbait a significant element in today's digital narrative.

The concept of clickbait isn't entirely new. It has its roots in traditional media practices, where catchy headlines and sensational stories were used to boost newspaper sales and television ratings. However, in the digital realm, clickbait has taken on a new dimension. The Internet's vast landscape, combined with the advent of social media, has created an environment where clickbait can thrive, reaching vast audiences with unprecedented speed and efficiency.

One of the critical aspects of clickbait is its reliance on human psychology. Clickbait headlines often play on our natural curiosities, fears, and desires, exploiting cognitive biases to draw us into clicking. The emotional pull of these headlines can be powerful, often overriding rational judgment and leading to a cycle of compulsive clicking that prioritizes sensationalism over substance.

The impact of clickbait goes beyond individual browsing habits. It has significant implications for journalism, content creation, and the dissemination of information. The rise of clickbait has sparked debates about media ethics, the quality of online content, and the balance between attracting audience attention and maintaining journalistic integrity. Furthermore, in an age where 'fake news' and misinformation are of growing concern, the role of clickbait in shaping public perception and discourse is a critical area of exploration.

"A Study of ClickBait" is structured to guide the reader through these various dimensions, offering insights from experts, analyses of real-world examples, and discussions of emerging trends and technologies. Whether you are a media professional, a student of communication, or simply a curious reader, this book aims to provide a nuanced understanding of clickbait and its place in our digital world.

As we embark on this journey, it is important to approach the topic of clickbait not just with critical eyes but also with an openness to understand its complexities. Clickbait, in its many forms, challenges us to rethink our relationship with digital media, to question what we consume, and to consider the future we are shaping through our clicks and shares.

Personal Motivation For Writing The Book

My personal motivation for writing "A Study of ClickBait" stems from a blend of professional intrigue and personal experience in the dynamic world of digital media. As a long-time observer and participant in the digital landscape, I have witnessed firsthand the transformative impact of clickbait on our collective media consumption habits. This book is the culmination of my journey to understand and contextualize this phenomenon in the broader narrative of information exchange in the digital age.

Professionally, my background in media studies and journalism has provided me with a front-row seat to the seismic shifts in content creation and distribution brought about by the Internet. Over the years, I have seen the media industry grapple with the challenges and opportunities presented by digital platforms. The rise of clickbait, in particular, caught my attention as a significant factor influencing not just media economics but also public discourse and perception. This book is an extension of my desire to explore the nuances of this trend, moving beyond superficial judgments to a deeper understanding of its mechanisms and implications.

On a personal level, my motivation is fueled by the experiences we all share as consumers of digital content. Like many, I have found myself drawn to captivating headlines, only to be left unsatisfied by the content that followed. These experiences led me to question the nature of the content we are presented with online and the reasons we engage with it. I became increasingly curious about the psychological hooks of clickbait and how they tap into our innate desires and fears.

Moreover, as misinformation and sensationalism increasingly cloud the digital information landscape, I felt a responsibility to contribute to a more informed and discerning public discourse. This book is an effort to empower readers with knowledge, encouraging them to critically evaluate the content they encounter and understand the broader implications of their online engagements.

"A Study of ClickBait" is, therefore, more than just an academic endeavor; it is a personal mission to shed light on a pervasive yet often under-examined aspect of our digital lives. Through this book, I hope to offer readers a comprehensive perspective on clickbait, blending academic research with practical insights and fostering a more nuanced and critical approach to digital media consumption.

Overview Of The Content

"A Study of ClickBait" is structured to provide a comprehensive and multifaceted exploration of the clickbait phenomenon. The content is organized into chapters, each delving into different aspects of clickbait, from its psychological underpinnings to its broader impact on media and society. Here's an overview of what readers can expect throughout the book:

Chapter 1: Understanding Clickbait

This chapter introduces the concept of clickbait, providing a clear definition and examining its evolution. It sets the stage for the reader to understand the basic mechanics of how clickbait works and why it has become a staple in digital media.

Chapter 2: The History of Clickbait

We trace the origins of sensationalist content, from traditional media to the digital age. This historical perspective helps readers grasp how clickbait is not a new phenomenon but rather an evolved form of content presentation.

Chapter 3: The Mechanics of Clickbait

Here, we dissect the common strategies and techniques used in clickbait. This includes an analysis of headline construction, emotional triggers, and the use of imagery, providing insights into how clickbait captures attention.

Chapter 4: Clickbait and Consumer Psychology

This chapter delves into the psychological aspects of clickbait. It explores why clickbait is so effective in engaging audiences, discussing cognitive biases and emotional appeals.

Chapter 5: Clickbait in the Age of Social Media

Focusing on the role of social media, this chapter examines how platforms like Facebook and Twitter have amplified the spread and impact of clickbait. It also discusses how algorithms contribute to the visibility of clickbait content.

Chapter 6: The Impact on Journalism and Media

We explore the effects of clickbait on journalism and media, including the challenges it poses to journalistic integrity and the shift in media business models.

Chapter 7: Ethical and Legal Considerations

This chapter addresses the ethical dilemmas and legal issues surrounding clickbait, including debates on misinformation, deceptive advertising, and the balance between free speech and responsible reporting.

Chapter 8: Fighting Back Against Clickbait

Here, we discuss strategies for identifying and combating clickbait. This includes tools for readers and content creators, as well as initiatives by digital platforms to curb misleading content.

Chapter 9: The Future of Clickbait

The book looks ahead, speculating on the future of clickbait in the context of emerging technologies and changing media landscapes. This chapter encourages readers to think critically about what lies ahead.

Chapter 10: Beyond Clickbait

We conclude with a discussion on alternatives to clickbait, highlighting success stories and best practices for creating engaging yet ethical content.

Throughout "Study of ClickBait," the content is interspersed with case studies, expert interviews, and real-world examples. This approach ensures that the book is not only informative and insightful but also engaging and relevant to a wide range of readers. Whether you are a media professional, a student, or simply an interested reader, this book aims to deepen your understanding of clickbait and its place in our digital world.

Chapter 1: Understanding Clickbait

Defining Clickbait: Clickbait refers to a type of online content, particularly headlines, crafted with the primary intention of attracting attention and encouraging visitors to click on a link to a particular web page. It is characterized by its sensationalist, provocative, or misleading nature, designed to capitalize on human curiosity and emotional responses.

Differentiating Clickbait from Traditional Headline Writing and Content Presentation:

Sensationalism and Emotional Appeal:

Clickbait: Often uses exaggerated or sensational language to provoke curiosity or emotional reactions. Examples include "You Won't Believe What Happened Next!" or "This One Weird Trick Can Change Your Life!"

Traditional Headlines: Aim to summarize the content accurately and informatively, often avoiding sensational language. For instance, "Study Finds New Technique Effective in Treating Disease".

Misleading or Deceptive Nature:

Clickbait: May promise more than the article delivers or use ambiguous phrasing to mislead the reader about the content of the article.

Traditional Content: Strives to ensure that headlines and content are aligned, providing a clear expectation of what the reader will learn or understand from the article.

Use of Curiosity Gaps:

Clickbait: Creates a 'curiosity gap' by providing incomplete information in the headline, compelling the reader to click to find out more.

Traditional Content: Offers a more comprehensive overview in the headline, minimizing gaps between the reader's expectations and the actual content.

Focus on Virality and Shareability:

Clickbait: Often optimized for social media sharing, relying on emotional engagement or shock value to encourage virality.

Traditional Content: While shareability is considered, the primary focus remains on the quality and relevance of the content rather than its potential for virality.

Content Quality and Depth:

Clickbait: The content behind clickbait headlines may lack depth, be overly simplistic, or not provide the comprehensive information promised by the headline.

Traditional Content: Generally offers a depth of information, analysis, or storytelling that reflects the promise of the headline, meeting the reader's expectations for quality and substance.

In essence, clickbait is distinguished by its primary goal of driving web traffic and engagement through sensationalism and emotional manipulation, often at the expense of accuracy and content quality. In contrast, traditional headline writing and content presentation prioritize accuracy, informativeness, and alignment between the headline and the article's content.

Characteristics of Clickbait

Clickbait is identifiable by several key features that differentiate it from more traditional forms of online content. Understanding these characteristics can help users recognize clickbait and navigate digital media more critically.

Sensationalism

Exaggerated Claims: Clickbait often makes exaggerated claims to capture the user's attention quickly. These can include hyperbolic statements or over-the-top assertions that the content itself may not fully support.

Dramatization: Even mundane or ordinary content is often dramatized to appear more exciting or newsworthy than it actually is.

Provocative Language

Emotionally Charged Words: Clickbait headlines frequently use emotionally charged words and phrases designed to evoke strong responses such as shock, excitement, or outrage.

Urgency and Hyperbole: The language used in clickbait often implies urgency or extremity (e.g., "shocking," "incredible," "you won't believe").

Promise of Intriguing Content

Curiosity Gap: Clickbait headlines often provide just enough information to pique interest but leave out key details, creating a 'curiosity gap'. This tactic compels readers to click on the link to satisfy their curiosity.

Teasers: The headline may tease a surprising revelation or a shocking twist that the article supposedly contains, urging the reader to find out more.

Ambiguity and Misdirection

Vague or Incomplete Information: Many clickbait headlines are intentionally vague or use ambiguous phrasing, leading readers to speculate about the content of the article.

Misleading Implications: Sometimes, clickbait headlines imply a story or angle that is not actually covered or supported in the article.

Emotional Appeal

Targeting Emotions: Clickbait often targets basic human emotions such as fear, joy, or anger. This emotional appeal is designed to make the content more shareable on social media.

Relatability: Attempting to relate to the reader's personal experiences or emotions to create a sense of connection or relevance.

Visual Elements

Eye-Catching Thumbnails: Clickbait articles often use bold and attention-grabbing images or thumbnails that may or may not be directly related to the article content.

Captivating Graphics: The use of colorful and dramatic graphics or photos that exaggerate or sensationalize the topic being discussed.

In summary, clickbait is characterized by its use of sensationalism, provocative language, promises of intriguing content, ambiguity, emotional appeal, and striking visual elements. These features are designed to maximize engagement, often prioritizing clicks over content quality and accuracy.

Evolution of Clickbait

Early Forms: The Origins in Print Media and Advertising

The phenomenon of clickbait, while prominently associated with the digital age, has roots that extend far back into the history of print media and advertising. Understanding these early forms provides context for how clickbait has evolved over time.

Sensationalism in Print Media

Yellow Journalism: The precursor to modern clickbait can be traced back to the late 19th century with the rise of yellow journalism. This style of journalism emphasized sensationalism over facts, using eye-catching headlines and exaggerated stories to sell more newspapers.

Tabloid Newspapers: Following the trend set by yellow journalism, tabloid newspapers further popularized the use of sensational headlines and stories focused on scandal, gossip, and entertainment, often at the expense of rigorous journalism.

Advertising Tactics

Emotional and Sensational Appeals: Early advertising tactics often relied on sensational and emotional appeals to capture attention and persuade consumers. This strategy is akin to clickbait's approach of using provocative headlines to attract views.

Bait-and-Switch Techniques: In advertising, bait-and-switch tactics, where an attractive offer or product is advertised to lure customers but is not actually available or is replaced with something else, can be seen as an early form of clickbait.

Early Broadcast Media

Radio and Television Teasers: With the advent of radio and later television, similar tactics were used to retain audience attention. Programs often used teasers and sensational reports, especially before commercial breaks, to keep viewers and listeners engaged.

Influence of Print Advertisements

Headline Dominance: In print advertisements, the headline was crucial in attracting potential buyers. This led to the development of headline writing as a key skill, focusing on capturing attention quickly and effectively – a skill that is foundational in creating digital clickbait.

Pulp Magazines and Fiction

Sensational Covers and Stories: Pulp magazines, popular in the early to mid-20th century, often featured lurid and sensational cover art and storylines, designed to attract readers with the promise of adventure, romance, or mystery.

The early forms of clickbait in print media, advertising, and broadcast media set the stage for the kind of content strategies we see in the digital realm today. The evolution from sensationalist journalism and advertising tactics to digital clickbait highlights a consistent thread in media history: the pursuit of capturing and retaining audience attention through sensationalism and emotional appeal. Understanding this historical context enriches our comprehension of modern clickbait's characteristics and its impact on media consumption.

Adaptation to Digital Media: The Advent of the Internet Era

Early Online News: As traditional media outlets began to establish an online presence in the 1990s, the foundational tactics of print and broadcast media were adapted to the new digital environment. This was the dawn of digital clickbait, where headlines and content were optimized for the burgeoning world of web browsing.

The Influence of SEO: The rise of search engine optimization (SEO) marked a significant turning point in clickbait evolution. Content creators started crafting headlines and articles to rank higher in search engine results, often prioritizing catchy and sensationalist phrases to attract clicks.

The Birth of Viral Content

Social Media and Sharing: The explosion of social media platforms in the 2000s fundamentally changed how content was shared and consumed. Clickbait became a powerful tool for driving web traffic, as headlines and articles designed to be shareable and emotionally engaging gained prominence.

The Viral Loop: Articles and posts with clickbait headlines were more likely to go viral, creating a feedback loop where such content was more frequently produced and shared.

Maturation and Saturation of Clickbait

Sophistication in Techniques: As internet users became more accustomed to clickbait, content creators began employing more sophisticated techniques, blending traditional marketing tactics with psychological insights to craft even more compelling clickbait.

Saturation and User Fatigue: With the proliferation of clickbait across the web, a degree of user fatigue began to set in. This led to both a skepticism of sensationalist headlines and a gradual tuning out of such content by more discerning web users.

The Role of Algorithms and Monetization

Algorithm-Driven Content: The algorithms used by social media platforms and search engines, which prioritize user engagement, inadvertently fueled the growth of clickbait. Content that garnered clicks, likes, and shares rose to the top, driving creators to produce more of the same.

Monetization Strategies: The direct link between ad revenue and web traffic in the digital economy solidified clickbait as a key strategy for many content creators and marketers, looking to capitalize on the maximum number of clicks.

Adapting to Changing User Preferences and Platform Policies

Evolving User Expectations: As internet users become more sophisticated, there is a growing demand for authenticity and value in digital content. This has pushed some content creators to find a balance between engaging headlines and substantive content.

Platform Responses: In response to criticism, many social media platforms and search engines have begun adjusting their algorithms to reduce the prevalence of clickbait, promoting more quality-driven and authentic content.

The adaptation of clickbait to digital media represents a significant shift in content strategy driven by technological advancements, changing user behaviors, and economic incentives. From its early roots in sensationalist journalism to its current form shaped by the intricacies of the digital landscape, clickbait has continually evolved, reflecting the ongoing challenges and opportunities in capturing online attention.

Current Trends: Modern Clickbait TechniquesThe Nuances of Social Media Clickbait

Platform-Specific Tactics: Modern clickbait techniques are increasingly tailored to specific social media platforms, exploiting their unique features and audience behaviors. For instance, visually driven platforms like Instagram may use eye-catching images, while Twitter clickbait might rely on provocative or controversial statements to incite reactions and retweets.

Emotionally Resonant Content: Clickbait has become adept at leveraging emotional resonance, with content designed to evoke strong feelings like outrage, amusement, or sentimentality, thereby increasing the likelihood of shares and comments.

Personalization and Micro-Targeting

Data-Driven Clickbait: With access to vast amounts of user data, modern clickbait can be highly personalized, targeting individuals based on their interests, browsing history, and demographic information. This makes clickbait more relevant and tempting to each user.

Micro-targeting Techniques: Advanced analytics allow for micro-targeting, where clickbait content is tailored to very specific audience segments, increasing its effectiveness.

The Role of Headlines and Thumbnails

Curiosity-Inducing Headlines: Modern clickbait headlines often create a 'curiosity gap' by promising intriguing or shocking content without giving away the full story, compelling users to click for more information.

Manipulative Thumbnails: Thumbnails accompanying clickbait articles are carefully selected or designed to grab attention, often using out-of-context images, exaggerated visuals, or suggestive content.

Interactive and Immersive Clickbait

Interactive Clickbait: Some clickbait techniques involve interactive elements like quizzes, polls, or clickable slideshows, making the content more engaging and increasing the time users spend interacting with it.

Story-Driven Formats: Leveraging storytelling formats that promise a narrative journey can be a subtle form of clickbait, drawing users in with the promise of a compelling story or outcome.

Adaptation to Algorithm Changes

Algorithm-Aware Content: As social media platforms update their algorithms to penalize traditional clickbait, creators are adapting by developing content that aligns better with these new algorithms while still aiming to maximize user engagement.

Balancing Quality and Click-Worthiness: There is a growing trend towards balancing the need for click-worthy headlines with the provision of quality content, as both content creators and platforms seek to maintain credibility and user trust.

The Spread of Misinformation

Clickbait and Fake News: The intersection of clickbait with misinformation and 'fake news' has become a significant issue, with sensationalized or misleading headlines often contributing to the spread of false information.

User Awareness and Backlash: There is a growing awareness among users of the misleading nature of clickbait, leading to a certain level of backlash and demand for more authentic content.

Modern clickbait techniques, especially in the context of social media and viral content, reflect an intricate understanding of human psychology, technological capabilities, and the changing landscape of digital platforms. While the core principle of attracting user attention remains constant, the methods have become more sophisticated, personalized, and, in some cases, more ethically ambiguous, necessitating a continuous evolution of both user awareness and platform policies.

The Mechanics of Clickbait

Headline Techniques: The Art of Clickbait Headlines

Clickbait has transformed the craft of headline writing into an art form that expertly plays on human curiosity and emotion. At the heart of this transformation are several headline formulas that have proven exceptionally effective in garnering clicks and engagement.

Listicles: A staple of clickbait, listicle headlines such as "10 Shocking Facts You Didn't Know" combine the allure of organized information with the promise of easy, digestible content. They create a sense of anticipation and order, making the overwhelming flood of online information seem more manageable. The numbered format not only piques curiosity but also provides a clear expectation of the content's structure, which is psychologically appealing to readers.

Question-Based Headlines: Headlines that pose questions, like "What Happens Next Will Surprise You," play on natural human curiosity. They invite readers to discover the answer, tapping into the innate desire for knowledge and understanding. This technique often creates a curiosity gap, providing just enough information to intrigue the reader without revealing too much, making the click almost irresistible.

Teasers: Teaser headlines are adept at hinting at a story or revelation without giving away the core content. Phrases like "You Won't Believe Who Was Spotted Together!" or "This New Discovery Changes Everything" are examples. They suggest exciting information lies just a click away, tantalizing the reader with the promise of something groundbreaking or sensational.

Hyperbolic and Emotional Language: Clickbait headlines frequently employ hyperbolic and emotionally charged language to grab attention. Words like "shocking," "incredible," or "heartbreaking" are common. They aim to evoke an emotional response, whether it's excitement, anger, or empathy, thereby increasing the likelihood of engagement.

Urgency and Exclusivity: Some clickbait headlines create a sense of urgency or exclusivity, suggesting that the reader might miss out on something important or timely if they don't click immediately. Examples include "Act Now Before It's Too Late" or "Exclusive Look Inside the Royal Wedding." This technique plays on the fear of missing out (FOMO), a powerful motivator in today's fast-paced digital world.

The effectiveness of these clickbait headline techniques lies in their ability to tap into fundamental human psychology. They exploit our innate desires for knowledge, order, and emotional connection, making them highly effective in the digital landscape where attention is the most valuable currency. Understanding these techniques is crucial, not just for content creators looking to engage audiences, but also for consumers striving to navigate the online world more critically.

Visual Tactics: The Power of Visuals in Clickbait

In the realm of clickbait, visuals play an equally crucial role as headlines in capturing audience attention. The strategic use of images, thumbnails, and other visual elements significantly enhances the appeal of clickbait, tapping into the visual-centric nature of human perception.

Provocative and Eye-Catching Thumbnails: Clickbait articles often feature thumbnails that are either provocative or extraordinarily eye-catching. These images are carefully selected or crafted to create an instant emotional reaction, be it shock, curiosity, or amusement. For instance, a thumbnail showing a surprising or unexpected image can make users pause their scrolling and engage with the content. In some cases, these images may only be tangentially related to the article content but are effective in driving clicks.

Use of Bright Colors and Bold Text: Clickbait visuals frequently utilize bright colors and bold text to stand out in a crowded digital space. The human eye is naturally drawn to vibrant colors and clear contrasts, making these visuals more likely to grab attention in a sea of content. Bold text overlays on images often reiterate or supplement the headline, adding an additional layer of allure and urgency.

Misleading Visual Context: A common tactic in clickbait is to use images that provide a misleading context or promise a story different from what the article actually delivers. This tactic plays on the human tendency to make quick judgments based on visual information, leading users to click on the article to resolve the discrepancy between the image and their expectations.

Creating a Narrative Through Visuals: Some clickbait effectively uses visuals to start telling a story, compelling the viewer to click through to the content for the full narrative. This could be a sequential series of images in a slideshow format or a single intriguing image that hints at a larger story.

Multimedia Elements: Beyond static images, clickbait has evolved to include other multimedia elements like GIFs, short videos, or animations. These dynamic visuals are particularly effective on platforms where motion draws the user's eye, such as social media feeds or video-sharing sites.

The visual tactics employed in clickbait are a testament to the adage, "a picture is worth a thousand words." In the fast-paced digital environment, where capturing user attention is paramount, these visual strategies are key to the success of clickbait content. They not only enhance the allure of the headline but often serve as the primary hook for audience engagement, capitalizing on the instantaneous and powerful impact of visual stimuli. Understanding these tactics is vital for discerning users who wish to navigate the digital landscape with a more critical eye.

Content Structure: Content Structure in Clickbait Articles

Maximizing Engagement Through Strategic Structure

Clickbait articles are meticulously structured to maximize reader engagement and time spent on the page. This structuring goes beyond the headline and visuals, delving into how the content itself is organized and presented to keep the reader hooked.

The Hook and Lead: The opening of a clickbait article is designed to immediately grab attention - the 'hook'. This might be a provocative statement, a surprising fact, or a compelling question. Following this, the 'lead' or introduction often builds on the headline's promise, offering just enough information to keep readers engaged without giving away the full story. This technique plays on the reader's curiosity, encouraging them to continue reading for the details or resolution.

Teasing and Delayed Gratification: One of the hallmarks of clickbait content structure is the practice of teasing information and delaying gratification. Key information or the answer to a question posed in the headline may be strategically placed towards the end of the article. This encourages readers to scroll through the entire piece, thereby increasing time on page. The content in between is often filled with supplementary information, anecdotes, or related facts that maintain interest but don't fully satisfy the reader's initial curiosity.

Use of Lists and Bullet Points: Many clickbait articles utilize list formats or bullet points to break down information. This not only makes the content appear more digestible and organized but also plays into the reader's desire for easy-to-consume information. Each point in the list invites the reader to keep moving to the next, creating a sense of progression and engagement.

Incremental Revelation: The structure often involves incrementally revealing information, a tactic that keeps the reader engaged in a continuous quest for more. Each section or paragraph reveals a bit more, but not all, of the story or information, compelling the reader to continue in search of the complete picture.

Interactive and Visual Elements: To further enhance engagement, clickbait articles may include interactive elements like quizzes, polls, or embedded social media posts. These elements, along with additional visuals like images or videos interspersed throughout the text, can break up large blocks of content and keep the reader engaged.

The content structure of clickbait articles is a calculated approach to maximize reader engagement and time spent on the page. Through the use of hooks, teases, list formats, and incremental information revelation, these articles skillfully keep readers engaged from beginning to end. While effective in terms of engagement metrics, this structure often prioritizes the enticement of the reader over the delivery of substantive content, highlighting the challenges in balancing reader engagement with content value. Understanding these structural tactics is crucial for readers seeking to navigate digital content more critically and for content creators aiming to strike a balance between engagement and quality.

Psychology Behind Clickbait

Cognitive Biases: The Psychological Underpinnings of Clickbait

Exploiting Natural Human Curiosity

One of the core reasons clickbait is so effective lies in its ability to exploit natural human curiosity. Clickbait headlines and content are often structured to create a 'curiosity gap' or a sense of mystery, which triggers an innate desire for knowledge and understanding.

This gap between what we know and what we want to know leads to an almost irresistible urge to click and find out more. The human brain is wired to seek out this missing information, making clickbait an expert tool in leveraging this cognitive bias for digital engagement.

Overconfidence and the Illusion of Knowledge

Clickbait also plays on the cognitive bias of overconfidence, particularly the illusion of knowledge. People often overestimate their understanding of a subject, and clickbait headlines can exploit this by promising surprising or little-known information, tempting readers with the allure of gaining new insights or confirming their knowledge. The tactic of suggesting that readers might not know the full story, as seen in headlines like "The truth behind…" or "What you don't know about…", effectively piques interest and challenges the reader's sense of knowledge, driving them to click.

The Fear Of Missing Out (FOMO)

FOMO, or the fear of missing out, is another powerful psychological factor that clickbait taps into. In a world overflowing with information and constant updates, people often experience anxiety over the possibility of missing out on important, interesting, or entertaining content. Clickbait headlines often imply that not clicking on them might result in missing out on crucial information or an engaging experience. This fear of being out of the loop or not being part of a shared social experience can make clickbait particularly compelling, driving people to click to stay informed or connected.

The effectiveness of clickbait is deeply rooted in these cognitive biases. By understanding the psychological factors at play, including curiosity, overconfidence, and FOMO, we can better appreciate why clickbait continues to be a prevalent strategy in the digital world. This knowledge not only helps in recognizing and resisting clickbait but also sheds light on broader aspects of human psychology and information consumption in the digital age.

Emotional Triggers: The Driving Force Behind Clickbait

Harnessing the Power of Emotions

Clickbait's effectiveness largely hinges on its ability to tap into a wide range of human emotions, from excitement and curiosity to anger and amusement. By leveraging these emotional triggers, clickbait compels users to click through, often without a second thought. The underlying principle is simple yet powerful: people are more likely to engage with content that resonates with them on an emotional level.

Excitement and Curiosity: Clickbait often promises content that is exciting, shocking, or too intriguing to miss. Headlines like "You Won't Believe What Happened Next!" or "This Incredible Discovery Will Amaze You" play on the excitement and curiosity of the reader. This approach preys on the natural human tendency to seek out novel and thrilling experiences or information, making the offer of new, surprising insights irresistible.

Anger and Outrage: Another common tactic is to incite anger or outrage, as these intense emotions can significantly drive engagement. Headlines that highlight injustice, scandal, or controversy – "The Outrageous Scam You Need to Know About" or "Why This Decision Has Everyone Furious" – are particularly effective in this regard. They not only attract immediate attention but also encourage sharing, as people often use social media to express their feelings and rally others around a cause or viewpoint.

Amusement and Light-Heartedness: On the lighter side, clickbait also leverages humor and amusement. Quirky, funny, or heartwarming headlines are used to attract those seeking a break from more serious content. These might include playful teasers, puns, or references to popular culture, appealing to the reader's sense of fun and entertainment.

In the realm of clickbait, emotions are not just responses to content; they are tools expertly used to drive engagement. By understanding how clickbait leverages these emotional triggers, readers can become more discerning in their online interactions, recognizing when their emotional responses are being targeted for clicks. For content creators, acknowledging the power of emotions underscores the responsibility they hold in shaping public discourse and the importance of balancing emotional appeal with factual accuracy and ethical considerations.

User Engagement: The Impact of Clickbait on Online Behavior

Clickbait and User Interaction Dynamics

Clickbait significantly influences user behavior online, particularly in terms of click-through rates and sharing patterns. Its design is meticulously crafted to maximize these engagements, playing a pivotal role in the way users interact with digital content.

High Click-Through Rates: Clickbait headlines are engineered to pique interest and curiosity, often leading to high click-through rates (CTR). The allure of uncovering the unknown or being entertained by something sensational drives users to click on links, even when they suspect that the content might not meet their expectations. This behavior is a testament to the effectiveness of clickbait in capturing user attention in the crowded online space, where the battle for clicks is relentless.

Sharing Patterns and Virality: Beyond individual clicks, clickbait also significantly affects sharing patterns. Content that evokes strong emotional reactions, be it excitement, anger, or amusement, is more likely to be shared. Clickbait leverages this by creating headlines and content that are not just click-worthy but also share-worthy. Users often share clickbait to express emotions, to appear in-the-know, or to engage in online communities and conversations. This propensity for sharing clickbait content contributes to its virality, further amplifying its reach and impact.

The Ripple Effect of Clickbait on Engagement

The influence of clickbait extends beyond initial clicks and shares. Its widespread use and effectiveness have broader implications for user engagement across the digital landscape:

Engagement Metrics and Content Strategy: The success of clickbait in driving engagement metrics like clicks, shares, and time spent on the page has led many content creators and marketers to adopt similar strategies. This trend often prioritizes immediate engagement over content quality or value, influencing the overall content strategy of many online platforms and publishers.

User Experience and Perception: Regular exposure to clickbait can shape user expectations and perceptions of online content. While it can lead to temporary spikes in engagement, over time, it may also foster skepticism and click fatigue among users. This evolving user experience raises questions about the long-term effectiveness and sustainability of clickbait as a content strategy.

Clickbait's impact on user engagement is both profound and complex. While it is undeniably effective in driving clicks and shares in the short term, its long-term effects on user behavior and the quality of online discourse are more ambiguous. Understanding these dynamics is crucial not just for content creators and marketers but also for users navigating the digital world. It underscores the need for a balanced approach to content creation that respects user intelligence and fosters genuine engagement.

Perception and Reception of Clickbait

Audience Perceptions of Clickbait

Clickbait, while effective in garnering immediate attention, often garners mixed perceptions among audiences. On the one hand, its ability to engage and entertain is undeniable, making it a popular tool in the arsenal of digital content creators. On the other hand, the perception of clickbait is frequently marred by its association with deceptive practices and low-quality content.

Initial Attraction vs. Subsequent Disappointment: The primary allure of clickbait lies in its promise of intriguing, entertaining, or shocking content. However, this initial attraction can quickly turn to disappointment if the content doesn't deliver on its promise. This gap between expectation and reality often leads to a negative perception of clickbait as misleading or manipulative.

Skepticism and Mistrust: Regular exposure to clickbait can lead to increased skepticism among internet users. Over time, audiences may become wary of sensational headlines, perceiving them as red flags for dubious content. This skepticism can extend beyond individual articles, impacting trust in the platforms or publishers that frequently rely on clickbait.

Backlash Against Clickbait

The perceived deceptive nature of clickbait has led to a notable backlash, both from individual users and broader online communities.

User Backlash and Criticism: Online platforms often witness user backlash against clickbait. Users may express their discontent in comments or through direct feedback, criticizing the use of misleading headlines or the lack of substance in the content. This backlash is amplified by the communal nature of social media, where collective opinions and criticisms can quickly gain momentum.

Impact on Brand Reputation: For brands and content creators, reliance on clickbait can lead to long-term reputational damage. If audiences consistently feel misled, their trust in the brand diminishes, which can have lasting effects on audience loyalty and engagement. Brands that are frequently associated with clickbait may find it challenging to rebuild credibility and re-establish a genuine connection with their audience.

The perception and reception of clickbait by audiences highlight the delicate balance between attracting attention and maintaining credibility in the digital age. While clickbait strategies may provide short-term engagement benefits, they can also lead to long-term trust issues and audience alienation. Understanding this dynamic is crucial for content creators and platforms aiming to build and sustain a loyal and engaged audience base. It underscores the importance of ethical content practices that respect the intelligence and expectations of the audience.

Clickbait and Information Consumption

Influence on Reading Habits: The Clickbait Effect Reshaping Online Information Consumption

Clickbait has significantly influenced how people consume information online, notably impacting reading habits and patterns of interaction with digital content. This influence extends beyond the mere act of clicking on a sensational headline and permeates the broader behavior of online reading.

Promoting a Skimming Culture: In the age of clickbait, there is a tendency for readers to skim through content rather than engage deeply. Clickbait headlines often promise quick answers or sensational revelations, aligning with and reinforcing the habit of skimming. Readers, anticipating that the content might not fully deliver on its headline's promise, often skim through to glean the main points without investing time in thorough reading. This skimming culture can lead to a superficial understanding of topics and a preference for bite-sized, easily digestible information over in-depth analysis.

Selective Reading Based on Headlines: Clickbait also promotes selective reading habits, where decisions about which articles to read are based heavily on headlines. As headlines become increasingly sensationalized to attract clicks, they play a dominant role in guiding reader choices. This often results in readers bypassing potentially valuable content that lacks sensational headlines, while gravitating towards articles with provocative titles, regardless of their actual content quality or relevance.

The Long-Term Impact on Information Processing

The clickbait-driven transformation in reading habits has broader implications for how information is processed and understood in the digital landscape:

Attention Span and Depth of Understanding: The prevalence of clickbait contributes to shorter attention spans and a preference for quick, surface-level engagement with content. This shift can affect the depth of understanding and critical engagement with complex issues, as readers are conditioned to seek immediate gratification rather than deep comprehension.

Perpetuating the Cycle of Sensationalism: As audiences grow accustomed to clickbait-style headlines and content, there is a risk of perpetuating a cycle where sensationalism is expected and normalised. This cycle can influence the types of content produced and shared online, potentially overshadowing more substantive, less sensational journalism and writing.

The influence of clickbait on reading habits is a critical aspect of its broader impact on digital media culture. It not only affects individual engagement with content but also shapes collective expectations and behaviors regarding information consumption. Recognizing and addressing these influences is essential for fostering a more discerning and critically engaged online audience, capable of navigating the complex and often sensationalized landscape of digital information.

Quality of Information: The Debate Over Clickbait Content
Clickbait and the Compromise of Information Quality

The rise of clickbait has sparked an ongoing debate regarding the quality and reliability of information it presents. At the heart of this discussion is the conflict between the objective to attract clicks and the responsibility to provide accurate, valuable content.

Sensationalism vs. Substance: Clickbait often prioritizes sensationalism over substance, leading to content that may captivate but not necessarily inform. The allure of dramatic headlines often comes at the expense of nuanced or comprehensive reporting. As a result, while clickbait is effective in drawing in readers, it frequently disappoints in delivering depth and accuracy. The information presented can be oversimplified, exaggerated, or even misleading, catering more to emotional responses than informed understanding.

Reliability and Trustworthiness: The reliability of information in clickbait content is a major concern. In the pursuit of virality, clickbait can distort facts, present unverified claims, or omit crucial context. This practice not only misleads readers but also contributes to a broader erosion of trust in digital content. As audiences become more aware of these practices, skepticism towards sensationalized content grows, leading to a general wariness of information quality in online media.

The Counterargument: Clickbait as a Tool for Engagement

Despite the criticisms, some argue that clickbait can be a legitimate tool for engagement, drawing attention to important topics that might otherwise go unnoticed.

Engagement as a Gateway: Proponents of clickbait argue that it can act as a gateway, drawing readers into topics they might not have otherwise explored. From this perspective, clickbait serves as an initial hook that, when used responsibly, can lead to greater awareness and understanding of significant issues.

The Balance Between Attraction and Information: Some content creators strive to balance the allure of clickbait with the delivery of quality information. In these cases, engaging headlines are not necessarily misleading but are crafted to pique interest while still accurately representing the content. This approach seeks to reconcile the need for visibility in a crowded digital space with the ethical imperative to provide reliable information.

The debate over the quality of information in clickbait content highlights a fundamental tension in the digital media landscape. While the need to attract audience attention in a competitive online environment is understandable, it raises crucial questions about journalistic integrity and the responsibility to provide accurate, meaningful content. Navigating this terrain requires a nuanced approach that considers both the power of engagement and the imperative for trustworthy and informative content.

Summary of Key Points

The Intricacies of Clickbait in the Digital Era

In exploring the multifaceted world of clickbait, this chapter delved into various aspects that define and influence this prevalent online phenomenon. The discussion illuminated not just the mechanics of clickbait but also its broader implications in the digital landscape.

Characteristics of Clickbait: At its core, clickbait is marked by sensational headlines, emotionally charged language, and visuals designed to capture instant attention. The chapter highlighted how these elements work in tandem to create a strong impetus for readers to click and engage with the content, often at the expense of depth and accuracy.

Psychological Underpinnings: A significant focus was on the psychological aspects that make clickbait so effective. We examined how clickbait taps into cognitive biases such as curiosity, overconfidence, and the fear of missing out (FOMO), which drive user behavior online. This exploitation of innate human tendencies is central to the success of clickbait strategies.

Impact on User Engagement: The chapter also addressed how clickbait shapes user engagement, particularly in terms of click-through rates and sharing patterns. It noted that while clickbait effectively drives initial engagement, it often leads to user dissatisfaction and skepticism, impacting long-term trust in content sources.

Quality of Information: The ongoing debate about the quality and reliability of information presented in clickbait was a crucial part of the discussion. We explored the tension between attracting readers and maintaining informational integrity, highlighting the potential for clickbait to mislead or provide superficial coverage.

Audience Perception and Reception: Lastly, we touched upon how audiences perceive and react to clickbait. The chapter brought to light the growing backlash against perceived deceptive practices in clickbait, underscoring a rising demand for more authentic and substantive online content.

Conclusion

In summary, the chapter provided a comprehensive overview of clickbait, dissecting its components, psychological appeal, and consequent effects on digital media consumption. By understanding the intricacies of clickbait, readers and content creators alike can navigate the digital landscape more consciously, striking a balance between engaging content and ethical information dissemination.

Definition And Evolution Of Clickbait

Defining Clickbait

Basic Definition: At its simplest, clickbait refers to online content that is designed to attract attention and encourage users to click on a hyperlink. It typically employs sensational headlines or intriguing thumbnails that pique curiosity or provoke emotional responses.

Core Features: Key characteristics include hyperbolic, provocative, or misleading headlines, a focus on viral elements, and often a disconnect between the headline and the actual content of the article or page.

Evolutionary Journey

From Sensationalism to Digital Bait: Clickbait's roots can be traced back to sensationalist journalism, where newspapers used eye-catching headlines to increase sales. The term has evolved in the digital era to describe a similar practice online, adapted to the fast-paced nature of internet browsing.

The Rise of Digital Media: With the growth of digital platforms, especially social media, clickbait has become a prevalent tactic for driving web traffic. It has adapted to the metrics-driven world of online media, where clicks, shares, and engagement are key performance indicators.

Algorithmic Influence: The evolution of clickbait has been significantly influenced by the algorithms of major platforms like Facebook, Twitter, and Google. These algorithms often prioritize content that generates a high level of user engagement, inadvertently encouraging the spread of clickbait.

The Shift in Clickbait Strategies

Early Internet Era: In the early days of the internet, clickbait was more straightforward, often relying on sensational or misleading headlines.

Sophistication and Subtlety: Over time, clickbait strategies have become more sophisticated, incorporating psychological triggers and nuanced emotional appeals. This includes the use of storytelling elements, interactive content, and personalization to attract clicks in a more subtle manner.

Response to Criticism and Changes in Algorithms: As users and platforms have become more aware of and critical towards clickbait, there has been a shift towards more refined techniques. Content creators are constantly adapting to changes in social media algorithms and public sentiment, resulting in an ever-evolving landscape of clickbait strategies.

The definition and evolution of clickbait reveal a practice deeply ingrained in the fabric of digital media. Its development from sensational newspaper headlines to a sophisticated online engagement tool reflects broader changes in media consumption and the economics of attention in the digital age. Understanding this evolution is crucial for comprehending the subsequent chapters, which delve deeper into the mechanics, psychology, and impact of clickbait in our contemporary digital landscape.

The Psychology Of Attention In The Digital Age

The Nature of Digital Attention

Attention Economy: In the digital age, attention is a scarce commodity. With an overwhelming amount of information available, capturing and maintaining audience attention is critical. Clickbait thrives in this environment by promising quick, engaging content.

Fragmented Attention: Digital media consumers often exhibit fragmented attention spans, due to constant exposure to various stimuli. Clickbait capitalizes on this by offering content that seems easy to digest and visually appealing.

Psychological Triggers in Clickbait

Curiosity Gap: Clickbait often creates a curiosity gap by providing just enough information to intrigue readers but withholding enough to compel them to click. This taps into our natural desire for closure and resolution.

Emotional Engagement: Clickbait headlines frequently use emotional triggers, such as excitement, outrage, or humor, to connect with readers on a personal level and encourage clicks.

The Fear of Missing Out (FOMO): Clickbait also exploits the fear of missing out on important or exciting information, a sentiment that is prevalent in the rapid information exchange of social media.

The Role of Cognitive Biases

Confirmation Bias: Clickbait often aligns with readers' pre-existing beliefs or interests, making it more likely they will engage with the content.

Instant Gratification: The digital age has heightened the desire for instant gratification. Clickbait feeds into this by promising quick answers or entertainment.

Overconfidence Bias: Sometimes, clickbait plays on the overconfidence bias, where readers click on articles thinking they know what the content is about, only to find something different or more nuanced.

The Impact of Technology on Attention

Algorithmic Filtering: The algorithms used by social media and search engines prioritize content that is likely to engage users, often leading to the promotion of clickbait.

Notification and Feedback Loops: Digital platforms create continuous loops of notifications and feedback (likes, shares, comments), which not only distract but also incentivize users to seek out more clickbait content.

Adapting to the Digital Attention Span

Content Design: Content creators have adapted to the digital attention span by designing content that is easy to consume quickly, often using lists, bullet points, and eye-catching visuals.

Interactive Elements: To keep the digitally distracted user engaged, interactive elements like quizzes, polls, or clickable slideshows are often incorporated into clickbait content.

Understanding the psychology of attention in the digital age is crucial for comprehending the effectiveness of clickbait. It reveals how cognitive biases, emotional triggers, and the structure of digital platforms all play a role in shaping our online behavior. This insight sets the stage for exploring the more detailed aspects of clickbait in the following chapters, including its impact on journalism, ethics, and consumer behavior.

Clickbait & Traditional Headlines Distinction

Defining Traditional Headlines

Purpose and Style: Traditional headlines aim to summarize the main point or gist of an article in a clear, concise manner. They typically avoid sensationalism and strive to be informative and direct.

Journalistic Integrity: In traditional journalism, headlines are crafted to reflect the content accurately, adhering to journalistic standards of truthfulness, accuracy, and objectivity.

Characteristics of Clickbait Headlines

Sensationalism and Provocation: Clickbait headlines often use sensational or provocative language to pique interest. They may exaggerate or tease the content in a way that traditional headlines do not.

Curiosity and Ambiguity: Unlike traditional headlines that inform, clickbait headlines often leave out key details or use ambiguity to create a curiosity gap, compelling the reader to click to find out more.

Emotional Appeal: Clickbait frequently employs emotional triggers to engage readers, which is less common in traditional headline writing.

The Purpose of Each

Traffic Generation vs. Information Dissemination: The primary goal of clickbait is to generate clicks and traffic, which often correlates with advertising revenue. Traditional headlines, on the other hand, aim to inform the reader and encourage reading based on interest in the topic.

Engagement Metrics: Clickbait is often aligned with the goals of digital platforms where engagement (clicks, likes, shares) is a key metric, while traditional headlines focus more on conveying the news or content accurately.

The Evolution of Headline Writing

Influence of Digital Media: The rise of digital media has blurred the lines between clickbait and traditional headlines. Many reputable outlets have adopted elements of clickbait to compete in the attention economy while trying to maintain journalistic standards.

Balancing Act: There's an ongoing balancing act in digital journalism between maintaining credibility and maximizing reader engagement, leading to a new breed of headlines that combine traditional values with more engaging elements.

Impact on Reader Perception and Trust

Trust and Credibility: Clickbait can erode reader trust over time, especially when the content doesn't deliver on the headline's promise. Traditional headlines tend to build credibility but might struggle to capture attention in a crowded digital space.

Reader Fatigue: Excessive exposure to clickbait can lead to reader fatigue and skepticism, affecting how all headlines, even traditional ones, are perceived.

Conclusion

Understanding the distinction between clickbait and traditional headlines is crucial in the digital age. While they serve different purposes and have different impacts, the line between them is increasingly blurred as media outlets navigate the challenges of the digital economy. This distinction sets the stage for later discussions in the book about the implications of clickbait on journalism, ethics, and information quality.

Chapter 2: The History Of Clickbait

Early Beginnings in Sensationalism

Roots in Yellow Journalism: Explore the origins of clickbait in the sensationalist reporting of the 19th century, known as yellow journalism, which prioritized eye-catching headlines and lurid stories to boost newspaper sales.

Evolution Through Tabloid Journalism: Discuss how the tactics of yellow journalism persisted and evolved in tabloid journalism throughout the 20th century.

Transition to the Digital Age

The Internet Era: Examine how the advent of the internet and digital publishing in the late 20th and early 21st centuries created a fertile ground for clickbait. The shift from print to digital media reduced costs and increased the potential audience size.

The Role of Early Online News and Blogs: Delve into how early online news sites and blogs began to experiment with attention-grabbing headlines to drive web traffic.

Rise of Social Media and Viral Content

Social Media as a Catalyst: Analyze how the rise of social media platforms like Facebook, Twitter, and YouTube in the mid-2000s provided new avenues for clickbait to flourish, emphasizing shareability and viral potential.

Viral Content and Listicles: Discuss the emergence of websites that specialized in viral content, listicles, and quizzes, which used clickbait headlines to maximize shares and clicks.

The Era of Algorithm-Driven Content

Influence of Platform Algorithms: Explore how changes in social media and search engine algorithms began to prioritize content that engaged users, inadvertently boosting the prevalence of clickbait.

Adaptation and Sophistication: Discuss how content creators adapted to these algorithm changes, leading to more sophisticated forms of clickbait that were designed to outsmart algorithmic detection.

The Backlash and Call for Change

Reader Fatigue and Backlash: Address the growing reader fatigue and backlash against clickbait, as audiences began to recognize and resent deceptive or overhyped headlines.

Platform Responses: Examine the responses from social media platforms and search engines, which started implementing measures to reduce the spread of clickbait and prioritize quality content.

Current State and Trends

The Balancing Act: Discuss the current state of clickbait, where content creators are continually balancing the need for engagement with the desire to maintain credibility and reader trust.

Emerging Trends: Identify emerging trends in clickbait, such as the use of AI and machine learning to create personalized clickbait content, and the potential future trajectory of clickbait strategies.

Conclusion

Summarize the historical journey of clickbait, highlighting its adaptability and resilience. Reflect on the lessons learned from the past and how they might inform the future of content creation and consumption in the digital age.

Early Examples In Print And Broadcast Media

Sensationalism in Print Media

Yellow Journalism: The late 19th and early 20th centuries saw the rise of yellow journalism, a style characterized by sensationalized, exaggerated, or outright fabricated headlines and stories. Newspapers like William Randolph Hearst's 'New York Journal' and Joseph Pulitzer's 'New York World' competed fiercely for readership, often resorting to lurid and sensational headlines.

Tabloid Newspapers: In the early 20th century, tabloid newspapers emerged, continuing the tradition of eye-catching headlines and stories focused on scandal, crime, and gossip. These publications prioritized shock value and entertainment over factual reporting.

Broadcast Media and Teaser Tactics

Radio and Television: With the advent of radio and later television, similar tactics were used to capture and retain audience attention. News programs and talk shows often used teasers and sensational reports to keep viewers hooked, especially before commercial breaks or at the end of broadcasts.

The Influence of Advertising

Ad-Driven Strategies: Print and broadcast media, heavily reliant on advertising revenue, developed strategies to maximize audience engagement. This often meant using attention-grabbing headlines or teasers to ensure a larger audience, thereby increasing the value of their advertising space.

Pioneers of Sensationalist Content

Notable Examples: Highlight some key figures and publications that were pioneers in using sensationalist tactics. This could include discussion of specific sensational stories or stunts that grabbed public attention.

The Role of Competition: Competition among newspapers and later broadcast networks was a driving force in the evolution of these tactics. The pressure to outdo rivals often led to more sensational and attention-grabbing content.

Transitioning to the Digital Realm

Early Online News: As news and media began to shift online in the 1990s and early 2000s, the foundational tactics of print and broadcast media were adapted to the new digital environment. The need to attract clicks became even more pronounced with the rise of internet journalism.

The Birth of Clickbait: Discuss how the term "clickbait" came into existence as a way to describe online content that employed sensationalist tactics specifically designed to attract clicks, a direct evolution of the headline strategies used in traditional media.

Conclusion

The chapter concludes by bridging the gap between the early examples of sensationalism in print and broadcast media and the emergence of clickbait in the digital age. This historical perspective sets the stage for understanding how traditional media practices influenced and shaped the clickbait tactics that are prevalent in today's digital landscape.

Transition To Digital Media

The Emergence of Digital Platforms

Early Internet Era: In the 1990s, as the internet became increasingly accessible, traditional media outlets began establishing their online presence. This shift marked the beginning of a new era in content dissemination.

Digital Adaptation: Newspapers and magazines started to migrate their content online, but soon realized that the strategies effective in print did not directly translate to the digital realm. The need for adaptation to the digital audience's consumption habits became evident.

The Rise of Online News and Blogs

Online News Portals: Major newspapers and broadcast networks launched online versions, experimenting with various formats to attract and retain readership.

Blogging Revolution: The early 2000s saw the rise of blogs and independent online platforms. These offered more personalized and niche content, often using engaging and provocative headlines to draw in readers.

The Click Economy

Clicks as Currency: In the digital media landscape, clicks became the new currency. The success of an article or a piece of content began to be measured by the number of clicks it generated, leading to the birth of click-driven journalism.

SEO and Visibility: The importance of search engine optimization (SEO) grew, as visibility on search engines like Google started to dictate web traffic. This led to headline strategies that were optimized for clicks and search engine algorithms.

The Changing Nature of Headlines

From Informative to Enticing: Unlike traditional headlines that aimed to inform, digital headlines increasingly aimed to entice. The goal shifted from summarizing the story to provoking curiosity or an emotional response, compelling the user to click.

A/B Testing and Analytics: Digital platforms began using A/B testing and analytics to fine-tune headlines for maximum click-through rates, leading to the rapid evolution of clickbait techniques.

Social Media: A New Frontier

Social Media Explosion: With the advent of social media platforms like Facebook and Twitter, the distribution of news and content underwent another major shift. Shareability and viral potential became crucial factors.

The Viral Loop: Content that generated strong emotional reactions was more likely to be shared, creating a viral loop. This further incentivized the creation of clickbait content designed to tap into these emotional responses.

The Maturation of Digital Media

Balancing Act: Established media outlets struggled to find a balance between maintaining journalistic integrity and adapting to the click-centric digital economy.

Diversification of Content: Alongside clickbait, there was also a growth in long-form journalism and multimedia content online, offering a counterbalance to click-driven content.

Conclusion

The transition to digital media fundamentally altered the landscape of journalism and content creation. This chapter sets the stage for understanding how clickbait became entrenched in the digital ecosystem, preparing the reader for a deeper exploration of its mechanics, psychology, and impact in the subsequent chapters.

Key Milestones In The Evolution Of Online Clickbait

The Advent of Online Advertising

Late 1990s – Early 2000s: The introduction of online advertising models, such as pay-per-click (PPC) and banner ads, created a direct financial incentive to attract web traffic. This marked the beginning of websites crafting content specifically to draw clicks.

Rise of Search Engine Optimization (SEO)

Early 2000s: As search engines like Google gained prominence, mastering SEO became crucial for online visibility. Websites began optimizing headlines and content to rank higher in search results, often prioritizing catchiness and keyword density.

The Social Media Revolution

Mid-2000s: The emergence of social media platforms like Facebook and Twitter changed how content was shared and consumed. Virality became a key goal, with clickbait headlines playing a significant role in encouraging users to share content.

The BuzzFeed Effect

2010s: BuzzFeed popularized a new form of clickbait with its listicles and quizzes. Their success demonstrated the power of combining clickbait headlines with shareable, light-hearted content, setting a trend followed by many other outlets.

Facebook's Algorithm Changes

2015 – 2016: Facebook, recognizing the proliferation of clickbait on its platform, updated its algorithm to reduce the visibility of clickbait headlines. This move forced content creators to adapt, signaling a shift towards more quality-driven content.

The Fake News Epidemic

2016: The U.S. Presidential Election brought the issue of 'fake news' and misleading clickbait to the forefront. The role of clickbait in spreading misinformation led to increased scrutiny and calls for greater responsibility among content creators and platforms.

The YouTube Clickbait Phenomenon

Late 2010s: YouTube saw a surge in clickbait tactics, with creators using sensational thumbnails and titles to attract views. This trend highlighted the extension of clickbait beyond text to visual media.

The Rise of Personalized Clickbait

Late 2010s – Early 2020s: Advanced algorithms and data analytics enabled the creation of personalized clickbait, tailoring headlines and content to individual users' preferences and browsing history, making clickbait more sophisticated and harder to discern.

Anti-Clickbait Measures and Reader Awareness

Early 2020s: Increased reader awareness and backlash against clickbait led to the rise of anti-clickbait tools and browser extensions. Media literacy campaigns also began emphasizing the importance of recognizing and avoiding clickbait.

The Ongoing Evolution

Present Day: The landscape of clickbait continues to evolve with new technologies and changing social media algorithms. The balance between attracting audience attention and maintaining content integrity remains a dynamic and ongoing challenge.

Conclusion

These key milestones highlight the adaptability and resilience of clickbait tactics in response to technological advancements and changing consumer attitudes. Understanding this evolution is crucial for grasping the current state of online media and the challenges that lie ahead in the digital information ecosystem.

Chapter 3: The Mechanics Of Clickbait

Introduction to Clickbait Mechanics

Overview: Setting the stage for a deep dive into the nuts and bolts of how clickbait works. This chapter aims to unpack the strategies and techniques that make clickbait effective in capturing attention and driving traffic.

Headline Techniques

The Curiosity Gap: Exploring how clickbait headlines are crafted to create a gap between what the reader knows and what the reader wants to know, compelling them to click for more information.

Emotional Triggers: Analysis of how clickbait headlines often use emotionally charged words and phrases to elicit strong responses, such as excitement, outrage, or amusement.

Use of Hyperbole and Sensationalism: Discussing the role of exaggeration and sensationalism in making mundane topics seem extraordinary.

Question-Based and Listicle Headlines: Understanding why headlines that pose questions or offer lists (e.g., "Top 10...") are particularly effective in clickbait.

Visual Tactics

Thumbnail Images: Examining how clickbait often uses provocative or misleading images as thumbnails to grab viewer attention.

Color and Design Elements: Discussing the importance of vibrant colors and eye-catching design in making clickbait visually appealing.

Content Structure

The Hook and Tease: Exploring how the opening lines of clickbait articles are designed to immediately grab attention and encourage further reading.

Narrative and Formatting Techniques: Analysis of how clickbait content is often formatted for easy consumption, using short paragraphs, bolded text, and bullet points.

The Payoff (or Lack Thereof): Discussing the common practice in clickbait of delaying the promised information or providing it in a less satisfying way than the headline suggested.

Engagement and Sharing

Emphasizing Shareability: Understanding the strategies used to make clickbait highly shareable on social media platforms.

Calls to Action: Examining how clickbait often includes direct calls to action, encouraging readers to engage with the content through likes, shares, or comments.

The Role of Algorithms

Algorithmic Optimization: Discussing how clickbait is tailored to perform well within the algorithms of major social media platforms and search engines.

Adaptive Strategies: Analysis of how clickbait creators continuously adapt their strategies in response to changes in algorithms.

Ethical Considerations

Balancing Engagement with Integrity: Exploring the ethical line between creating engaging content and misleading readers.

Impact on Reader Trust: Discussing the long-term impact of clickbait tactics on reader trust and the credibility of information sources.

Conclusion

Summarizing the key mechanics of clickbait and reflecting on the implications for content creators and consumers. This chapter aims to equip readers with the knowledge to not only identify clickbait but also understand the rationale behind its construction.

Analysis Of Common Clickbait Strategies

The Curiosity Gap

Definition and Implementation: The curiosity gap is a tactic where the headline promises intriguing information but leaves out key details, creating a gap between what the reader knows and what they are curious to find out.

Psychological Basis: This strategy exploits the natural human tendency to seek closure or resolution to an incomplete story or idea.

Examples in Action: Analyzing real-world examples of curiosity gap headlines, showing how they provoke questions that can only be answered by clicking on the link.

Emotional Appeal

Leveraging Emotions: Emotional appeal in clickbait involves crafting headlines that trigger strong emotional responses, such as excitement, anger, or amusement.

Connection to Sharing Behavior: Emotionally charged content is more likely to be shared on social media. This section explores how clickbait creators use this knowledge to increase the viral potential of their content.

Case Studies: Presenting case studies that demonstrate how emotional appeal is used in clickbait headlines and the impact on user engagement.

The Use of Hyperbole

Exaggeration as a Tool: Hyperbole involves exaggerating or overstating aspects of the story to make it seem more extraordinary or urgent than it actually is.

Impact on Reader Expectations: Discussing how hyperbole can lead to inflated expectations, often resulting in disappointment when the actual content is revealed.

Shock Value

Shock as a Hook: Analyzing how clickbait often uses shocking or controversial statements or images to grab attention.

The Fine Line: Exploring the ethical considerations and potential backlash associated with using shock value, including the desensitization of audiences over time.

Personalization and Relatability

Tailoring Content to Audiences: Discussing how clickbait creators often craft content that appears personally relevant or relatable to target demographics.

Use of Data and Analytics: Exploring how data analytics are used to personalize clickbait, increasing its effectiveness.

Novelty and Uniqueness

The Allure of the New: Examining how clickbait headlines often promise new, groundbreaking, or exclusive information, tapping into the audience's desire for novel content.

Balancing Novelty with Credibility: Discussing how the promise of novelty can sometimes stretch the bounds of credibility, leading to skepticism among more discerning readers.

Conclusion

This analysis of common clickbait strategies reveals a complex interplay between psychology, technology, and media economics. Understanding these strategies not only helps in identifying clickbait but also sheds light on the broader dynamics of content consumption in the digital age.

The Role Of Headlines And Visuals

Headlines: The Primary Hook

The headline is the most critical element of clickbait. It serves as the initial point of contact with the audience and is strategically crafted to capture attention instantly. Clickbait headlines typically use powerful, emotive language and often include elements of mystery, shock, or intrigue. They are designed to tap into the reader's curiosity, encouraging them to seek closure or resolution by clicking on the link. The success of a clickbait article heavily relies on the effectiveness of its headline in creating an irresistible urge to know more.

Visual Elements: Enhancing the Appeal

Visuals play a complementary yet crucial role in reinforcing the impact of clickbait headlines. Images, gifs, or videos associated with clickbait are often provocative, unusual, or emotionally charged. These visuals are selected to create an immediate emotional connection or response, enhancing the overall allure of the content. The right visual can amplify the headline's message, making the content more appealing and shareable.

Synergy Between Headlines and Visuals

The combination of a compelling headline and an engaging visual creates a powerful synergy. This dual appeal works to capture both the readers who respond more to textual cues and those who are more influenced by visual stimuli. In the realm of social media, where scrolling quickly through feeds is the norm, this synergy becomes even more critical. The headline and visual must work together seamlessly to stand out amidst a sea of competing content.

The Evolution of Headlines and Visuals in Clickbait

Over time, the use of headlines and visuals in clickbait has evolved. Initially, the focus was largely on sensational headlines, but as the digital landscape became more visually oriented, particularly with the rise of platforms like Instagram and Pinterest, the role of visuals gained prominence. Today, the most effective clickbait often combines a captivating headline with an equally compelling visual, each element reinforcing the other to maximize the content's impact.

The Impact on User Engagement

The effectiveness of headlines and visuals in clickbait is ultimately measured by user engagement. Click-through rates, shares, likes, and comments are all metrics used to gauge this engagement. Clickbait that skillfully combines an intriguing headline with an engaging visual tends to perform better on these metrics. However, this focus on engagement can sometimes lead to a compromise in content quality or accuracy, a topic that is critically examined in later chapters.

Conclusion

Understanding the role of headlines and visuals in clickbait is essential for comprehending its mechanics and its pervasive presence in digital media. This chapter sets the foundation for deeper discussions on the ethical implications and the impact of clickbait on media consumption and public discourse.

Case Studies Of Successful Clickbait Campaigns

Case Study 1: BuzzFeed's Mastery of Listicles and Quizzes

Overview: BuzzFeed, particularly in the early 2010s, became synonymous with clickbait through its innovative use of listicles and quizzes.

Strategy: Their strategy involved creating content that was easily consumable, highly shareable, and often lighthearted or humorous. Headlines were crafted to spark curiosity and engagement, such as "10 Things You Never Knew About Cats" or "Which Harry Potter Character Are You?"

Impact: These articles and quizzes went viral on social media, driving significant web traffic and user engagement. BuzzFeed's approach not only popularized the listicle format but also set a benchmark for viral content online.

Case Study 2: Upworthy's Emotional Headlines

Overview: Upworthy, a website launched in 2012, became known for its emotionally charged headlines designed to tug at the heartstrings or spark outrage.

Strategy: The site focused on curating feel-good stories, social issues, and inspirational content. Their headlines were often long and highly emotive, such as "Watch a Man's Life Change in Just 2 Minutes, Thanks to a Text".

Impact: Upworthy's headlines successfully capitalized on the emotional appeal, leading to high levels of engagement and widespread sharing, particularly on Facebook. Their approach demonstrated the power of emotional storytelling in the digital age.

Case Study 3: The Dodo's Animal-Focused Content

Overview: The Dodo, a digital media brand focused on animals, leveraged clickbait to attract a vast audience of animal lovers.

Strategy: Their content strategy combined adorable or heartwarming animal videos with headlines that played on the viewers' emotions and curiosity, such as "This Dog Can't Believe Her Dad Finally Found Her After 6 Months."

Impact: This approach resonated strongly with social media users, leading to high engagement rates. The Dodo's success highlighted how niche content, when paired with effective clickbait tactics, can build a dedicated and engaged audience.

Case Study 4: Playbuzz's Interactive Content

Overview: Playbuzz excelled in creating interactive content that went beyond traditional articles, incorporating quizzes, polls, and slideshows.

Strategy: Their clickbait strategy involved crafting headlines that promised a fun, interactive experience, often personalized to the user's interests or identity.

Impact: Playbuzz's content saw high levels of engagement and time spent on the page, proving that interactivity combined with clickbait headlines can lead to deeper user engagement.

Conclusion

These case studies demonstrate the diverse approaches to clickbait across different content platforms. From BuzzFeed's listicles to Upworthy's emotional narratives, each case study provides insights into the tactics that made these campaigns successful. They also underline the broader implications of clickbait in terms of user engagement, content strategy, and the evolving landscape of digital media.

Chapter 4: Consumer Psychology

Clickbait and Consumer Psychology

Introduction to Consumer Psychology in Digital Media

This chapter opens with an overview of how consumer psychology plays a pivotal role in the effectiveness of digital media, particularly in the realm of clickbait. It sets the stage for understanding the psychological underpinnings that make clickbait so appealing to a wide array of internet users.

The Science Behind the Click

An exploration of the psychological mechanisms that clickbait taps into. This includes an analysis of cognitive biases such as the curiosity gap, where incomplete information leads to a natural desire to seek out the missing pieces, or the fear of missing out (FOMO), which drives individuals to stay continually connected and informed.

Emotional Triggers in Clickbait

This section delves into how clickbait effectively utilizes emotional triggers to engage consumers. It examines the types of emotions most commonly exploited by clickbait, such as excitement, anger, or humor, and how these emotions influence online behavior, including clicking and sharing content.

The Role of Curiosity and Novelty

Curiosity is a powerful motivator in human behavior, and clickbait headlines often exploit this by promising new, surprising, or exclusive information. This section explores how the allure of novelty and the promise of new knowledge can override rational decision-making and lead to increased engagement with clickbait.

Behavioral Patterns in Clickbait Consumption

An analysis of the typical behavioral patterns exhibited by consumers when interacting with clickbait. This includes impulse clicking, where decisions are made rapidly without much thought, and the tendency for repeated engagement, where users continually fall for clickbait despite being aware of its nature.

The Impact of Social Influence

Understanding the role of social influence in the spread of clickbait is crucial. This part examines how social norms, peer influence, and the desire for social belonging affect the way individuals interact with and share clickbait content.

Personalization and Targeting in Clickbait

With the advent of sophisticated data analytics, clickbait has become more personalized and targeted. This section discusses how consumer data is used to tailor clickbait to individual preferences and interests, making it more effective and harder to resist.

The Psychological Cost of Clickbait

While clickbait can be seen as a harmless marketing tool, this section addresses the potential psychological costs, including misinformation, decreased trust in media, and the effect on mental health due to constant exposure to sensationalized content.

Conclusion

The chapter concludes by summarizing how a deeper understanding of consumer psychology can not only help in recognizing and resisting clickbait but also offers insights into the broader implications of how we consume information in the digital age. This understanding is crucial for consumers, content creators, and policymakers alike in navigating the complex landscape of digital media.

Understanding The Psychological Triggers

The Power of Curiosity

Curiosity is a fundamental human instinct, and clickbait headlines often exploit this by hinting at information that seems both intriguing and incomplete. This tactic creates a 'curiosity gap,' compelling the reader to click on the link to satisfy their curiosity. The effectiveness of this strategy lies in its ability to tap into the natural human desire for knowledge and closure.

Leveraging Fear and Anxiety

Fear-based triggers, such as warnings or alarming statements, are frequently used in clickbait to create a sense of urgency or danger. These headlines often play on common anxieties or phobias, driving clicks through a psychological need to alleviate these fears or to be informed about potential threats.

The Role of Excitement and Anticipation

Clickbait also capitalizes on positive emotions like excitement and anticipation. Headlines that promise entertainment, joy, or surprise can be highly effective. This type of clickbait often includes teasers about uplifting stories, amazing discoveries, or exciting offers, tapping into the human tendency to seek out pleasurable experiences.

Exploiting the Fear of Missing Out (FOMO)

FOMO is a particularly potent trigger in the age of social media, where there is a constant flow of information and a fear of not being in the know. Clickbait headlines often hint at information or experiences that everyone is talking about, leveraging the social anxiety of being left out of the loop.

The Appeal to Emotions and Empathy

Many clickbait headlines draw on emotional and empathetic responses. These can range from heartwarming stories to outrage-inducing reports. The emotional pull of these headlines makes them highly shareable, as people often engage more with content that resonates with them on an emotional level.

The Intrigue of Mystery and Surprise

Humans have a natural affinity for mystery and surprise, and clickbait often capitalizes on this by promising unexpected twists or shocking revelations. This type of content plays on the pleasure people derive from experiencing the unexpected and the joy of discovering something new.

Conclusion

Understanding these psychological triggers is key to both recognizing clickbait and comprehending its widespread appeal. By tapping into fundamental human emotions and instincts like curiosity, fear, excitement, and the desire for social inclusion, clickbait can effectively draw in a wide range of audiences. This understanding also highlights the challenges faced in balancing engaging content with ethical considerations in the digital media landscape.

Behavioral Economics Perspectives

Instant Gratification

In the realm of behavioral economics, instant gratification plays a significant role in the appeal of clickbait. Digital media consumers often seek immediate rewards, and clickbait headlines promise quick and easy access to interesting or valuable information. This aligns with the tendency of individuals to prefer smaller, immediate payoffs over larger rewards that require a wait, a concept known as hyperbolic discounting.

Decision Fatigue

Decision fatigue refers to the deteriorating quality of decisions made by individuals after a long session of decision making. In the context of clickbait, the overwhelming amount of content available online can lead to decision fatigue, making users more susceptible to clickbait. Simple, eye-catching headlines can become more appealing as they require less cognitive effort to process in a state of decision fatigue.

Loss Aversion

Another relevant concept is loss aversion, the idea that people prefer to avoid losses rather than acquire equivalent gains. Clickbait often frames information in a way that taps into this fear of missing out on something important, compelling users to click on the link to avoid the perceived loss of not being informed.

The Paradox of Choice

The paradox of choice in behavioral economics suggests that an abundance of choices can lead to anxiety and indecision. In the context of clickbait, when faced with a multitude of content options, a sensational or provocative headline can stand out, simplifying the decision-making process and making it more likely for a user to engage with the clickbait content.

Anchoring Effect

Clickbait can also be understood through the lens of the anchoring effect, where individuals rely too heavily on the first piece of information offered (the "anchor") when making decisions. In digital media, a sensational headline can serve as an anchor, influencing how the subsequent information is perceived and often leading to a skewed interpretation of the content.

Social Proof

Social proof is a psychological and social phenomenon where people copy the actions of others in an attempt to undertake behavior in a given situation. Clickbait often uses indicators of social proof, such as the number of shares or likes, to persuade more users to click, based on the assumption that if many others have engaged with the content, it must be worthwhile.

Conclusion

The principles of behavioral economics provide a deeper understanding of why clickbait is so effective. By leveraging aspects like instant gratification, decision fatigue, loss aversion, the paradox of choice, anchoring effect, and social proof, clickbait creators can skillfully manipulate online behavior. This perspective not only helps in analyzing the success of clickbait but also raises important questions about consumer autonomy and the ethical dimensions of content creation in the digital age.

The Impact Of Clickbait On Reader Emotions And Actions

Emotional Engagement and Clickbait

Clickbait's effectiveness largely hinges on its ability to evoke strong emotional responses. Whether it's curiosity, amusement, shock, or outrage, these emotional triggers are strategically used to capture attention and prompt immediate action, typically in the form of clicking or sharing. This emotional engagement is a double-edged sword; it can lead to increased interaction and engagement with content but can also result in emotional manipulation, where readers are drawn into content that may not deliver on its emotional promise.

Reader Actions Driven by Emotions

Clicking and Sharing: The initial emotional response elicited by a clickbait headline often leads to impulsive clicks. Additionally, the nature of the content, often surprising or sensational, increases the likelihood of it being shared, as users are motivated to elicit similar emotional responses in their social circles.

Commenting and Discussing: Emotional engagement can also lead to increased commenting and discussion, particularly with content that evokes polarizing opinions or strong reactions. This not only drives further engagement but also contributes to the content's visibility and reach.

The Cycle of Anticipation and Disappointment

Expectation vs. Reality: Clickbait often sets up an expectation through its headline, which may not be fulfilled by the actual content. This can lead to a cycle of anticipation and disappointment, where readers' initial excitement or curiosity turns into dissatisfaction.

Impact on Trust and Credibility: Repeated experiences of such disappointment can erode trust in certain content sources, potentially leading to a broader skepticism towards online media.

Psychological Consequences of Persistent Clickbait Exposure

Desensitization: Over time, regular exposure to sensationalized or exaggerated content can lead to desensitization, where readers become less responsive to emotional triggers.

Information Overload and Fatigue: The constant bombardment of clickbait can contribute to information overload and fatigue, making it harder for individuals to engage deeply or thoughtfully with content.

Behavior Modification and Habit Formation

Habituation to Clickbait: Regular interaction with clickbait can lead to habit formation, where users unconsciously seek out and click on sensationalized content, reinforcing the cycle of clickbait consumption.

Altered Content Preferences: Long-term exposure to clickbait can also alter content preferences, with readers becoming more inclined towards sensational or superficial content, potentially at the expense of more substantive material.

Conclusion

The impact of clickbait on reader emotions and actions is profound and multifaceted. While it can drive engagement and make content viral, it also raises concerns about emotional manipulation, the quality of reader experiences, and the long-term effects on media consumption habits. Understanding these impacts is crucial for content creators, consumers, and platforms alike, as they navigate the complexities of emotion-driven content in the digital landscape.

Chapter 5: Clickbait In The Age Of Social Media

Introduction: The Convergence of Clickbait and Social Media

This chapter begins by illustrating how the rise of social media has created an ideal ecosystem for clickbait to thrive. It explores the symbiotic relationship between clickbait tactics and the nature of social media platforms, where engagement and shareability are paramount.

Amplification of Clickbait Through Social Media

Viral Nature of Content: Delving into how social media platforms are designed to facilitate the rapid spread of content, making them fertile ground for clickbait. The viral nature of clickbait is enhanced by features like sharing, liking, and commenting.

Algorithmic Promotion: Understanding how social media algorithms often prioritize content that generates high engagement, inadvertently favoring clickbait. This section looks at how the quest for likes, shares, and comments influences content visibility.

The Role of User Psychology in Social Media Clickbait

Social Validation and Sharing: Examining the psychological factors that drive users to share clickbait on social media, including the desire for social validation and the urge to be part of trending conversations.

Echo Chambers and Filter Bubbles: Discussing how clickbait contributes to the formation of echo chambers and filter bubbles on social media, where users are repeatedly exposed to similar types of sensationalized content.

Clickbait Strategies Tailored for Social Media

Headlines and Hashtags: Analyzing how clickbait headlines are crafted specifically for social media, often using trending keywords and hashtags to increase visibility and engagement.

Visual Clickbait in Social Media: Exploring the use of eye-catching images, GIFs, and videos as forms of visual clickbait on platforms like Instagram and TikTok.

The Impact on Social Media Users and Discourse

Influence on Public Opinion and Discourse: Investigating the impact of clickbait on shaping public opinion and discourse on social media, particularly in regards to controversial or polarizing topics.

Desensitization and Mistrust: Addressing the potential for desensitization to sensationalized content among social media users and the consequent erosion of trust in online information sources.

Platform Responses and Evolving Tactics

Measures Against Clickbait: Exploring the steps taken by social media platforms to combat the spread of clickbait, such as algorithm adjustments and the introduction of fact-checking features.

Adaptation by Content Creators: Discussing how content creators adapt to these measures, continually evolving their clickbait strategies to maintain visibility and engagement on social media platforms.

Conclusion

Concluding the chapter, a reflection on the ongoing evolution of clickbait within the ever-changing landscape of social media. This section contemplates future trends, challenges, and the potential for a more balanced coexistence between engaging content and responsible social media usage.

The Role Of Social Media Platforms In Propagating Clickbait

Social media platforms play a pivotal role in the propagation of clickbait, acting as accelerators and amplifiers of content that is designed to attract maximum attention and engagement. The very nature of these platforms, with their emphasis on quick consumption and sharing of information, creates an environment where clickbait can thrive.

Acceleration of Content Spread

Social media platforms are designed for rapid information dissemination, making them ideal for spreading clickbait. Content that is catchy, controversial, or emotionally charged – typical characteristics of clickbait – is more likely to be shared and spread rapidly across networks.

The design of social media feeds, where users can easily scroll and interact with a variety of content, lends itself to the quick consumption of clickbait headlines.

Algorithmic Amplification

Most social media platforms use algorithms that prioritize content based on engagement metrics like clicks, shares, and time spent on content. Clickbait, often generating high engagement, is thus favored by these algorithms and gains increased visibility.

The algorithms also track user behavior and preferences, which can lead to personalized feeds where clickbait content is more likely to appear if it aligns with a user's previous interactions.

The Role of User Interaction

User interactions on social media, such as likes, comments, and shares, not only signal to the algorithm the popularity of content but also contribute to its wider dissemination. Clickbait headlines are often designed to provoke such interactions, whether through curiosity, controversy, or emotional reactions.

The ease of sharing content on social media means that clickbait can reach a broad audience quickly, far beyond the original publisher's own followers.

The Impact on Content Quality and Perception

The prevalence of clickbait on social media can lead to an overall decline in the quality of information, as sensational or misleading headlines overshadow more substantive content.

Continuous exposure to clickbait on these platforms can also affect users' perception of news and information, potentially leading to skepticism or mistrust towards online content in general.

Social media platforms, with their vast reach and influential algorithms, play a significant role in the spread and impact of clickbait. Understanding this role is essential in addressing the challenges posed by clickbait and in navigating the evolving landscape of digital content consumption.

How Algorithms Favor Clickbait Content

In the digital media landscape, algorithms play a critical role in shaping what content we see and interact with. These algorithms, particularly those used by social media platforms and search engines, often inadvertently favor clickbait content due to their underlying mechanics and the metrics they prioritize.

Engagement-Based Algorithms

Many social media platforms use engagement-based algorithms, which prioritize content that garners a lot of clicks, likes, comments, and shares. Clickbait headlines are particularly adept at triggering these forms of engagement, often through emotional appeals or curiosity-inducing teasers. As a result, content with clickbait headlines is more likely to get a higher ranking in users' feeds.

The Role of User Behavior in Algorithmic Decisions

Algorithms are designed to cater to user interests and behaviors. When users frequently click on sensational or exaggerated headlines, the algorithm interprets this as a preference for such content and adjusts accordingly. This creates a feedback loop where clickbait content is more frequently presented to users, reinforcing their engagement with similar content.

Time Spent and Click-Through Rates

Beyond likes and shares, algorithms also consider the amount of time users spend on a piece of content and the click-through rate. Clickbait, by its nature, often has high click-through rates due to its compelling headlines. If the content effectively keeps users engaged, even for a short duration, it can signal to the algorithm that the content is worth promoting.

Personalization and Targeted Content

Modern algorithms are sophisticated enough to personalize feeds based on user data, including past interactions, search history, and demographic information. Clickbait creators often tailor their content to appeal to specific audiences, making their content more likely to be picked up and amplified by these personalized algorithms.

The Viral Potential of Clickbait

Algorithms also account for the potential virality of content. Clickbait headlines, which are often designed to be shareable and elicit strong reactions, have a higher likelihood of going viral. This virality feeds into the algorithm's propensity to distribute content widely, leading to a greater visibility of clickbait.

Conclusion

Algorithms, while designed to enhance user experience by showing relevant and engaging content, can inadvertently promote clickbait due to its high engagement nature. Understanding this dynamic is crucial for both consumers and creators of digital content, as it highlights the influence of algorithmic decision-making on online information consumption and the challenges it poses in ensuring a balanced and informative digital media environment.

The Social Dynamics Of Sharing Clickbait

The act of sharing clickbait on social media involves complex social dynamics, influenced by psychological factors, user behavior, and the nature of online communities. Understanding why and how clickbait is shared can provide insights into its widespread prevalence and the role it plays in digital communication.

Psychological Motivators for Sharing

Emotional Response: Clickbait often elicits strong emotional reactions, whether it's excitement, outrage, or curiosity. These emotions can drive users to share content as a way of expressing their feelings or inciting similar reactions in others.

Social Identity and Validation: Sharing content on social media can be a way for individuals to reinforce their social identity and beliefs. Clickbait articles that align with a user's views or interests are more likely to be shared as a form of self-expression and validation from their social network.

The Role of Group Dynamics

Echo Chambers: In online communities or networks where like-minded individuals interact, clickbait that conforms to the group's views or interests is more likely to be shared. This contributes to the formation of echo chambers, where similar ideas are amplified, reinforcing collective beliefs.

Viral Sharing in Communities: Some clickbait is shared widely within specific communities or groups due to its viral nature. A sensational or intriguing headline can spark discussions, debates, or even just amusement, leading to widespread sharing within the group.

The Impact of Platform Mechanics

Algorithmic Encouragement: Social media algorithms often promote content that is likely to engage users. As clickbait is designed to be engaging, it tends to be more visible and, as a result, more shareable.

Ease of Sharing: The design of social media platforms, where sharing content can be done with a simple click or tap, facilitates the rapid spread of clickbait. This ease of sharing plays a significant role in how quickly clickbait can circulate across networks.

The Influence of Current Events and Trends

Trendjacking: Clickbait creators often capitalize on current events, trends, or popular culture to craft headlines that are timely and relevant, increasing the likelihood of them being shared.

Information Cascades: In situations where a piece of clickbait becomes extremely popular, it can create an information cascade, where users share the content simply because they see others doing so, not necessarily because of the content's intrinsic value.

Conclusion

The social dynamics of sharing clickbait underscore the interplay between individual psychology, group behavior, and the technical aspects of social media platforms. This phenomenon reflects broader patterns of communication and interaction in the digital age, where the nature of content, as well as the context in which it is shared, plays a critical role in its spread and impact. Understanding these dynamics is key to comprehending the life cycle of clickbait and its influence on digital discourse.

Chapter 6: The Impact On Journalism And Media

Introduction: Clickbait's Influence on Modern Journalism

The chapter opens by setting the stage for the profound impact that clickbait has had on journalism and media. It examines how the rise of clickbait has not only influenced content strategies but also posed significant challenges and opportunities for traditional and digital media outlets.

Changing Newsroom Priorities

Traffic-Driven Journalism: Delve into how the pursuit of web traffic and social media engagement has shifted some newsrooms' focus towards clickbait-style content. This shift often emphasizes quantity over quality, with a focus on stories that are more likely to generate clicks.

Impact on Editorial Decisions: Explore how the prevalence of clickbait has influenced editorial decisions, potentially leading to sensationalism or the oversimplification of complex issues in an effort to attract a broader audience.

Economic Implications for Media Outlets

Advertising Revenue and Clickbait: Discuss how the ad-based revenue model of many online media outlets encourages the production of clickbait, as more clicks translate into more ad impressions and revenue.

The Dilemma of Quality vs. Profitability: Analyze the tension between maintaining journalistic integrity and the economic pressures to produce content that drives traffic and revenue.

The Effect on Journalistic Standards and Ethics

Dilution of Journalistic Standards: Consider how the pressure to create clickbait can lead to a dilution of traditional journalistic standards, including accuracy, objectivity, and depth of reporting.

Ethical Concerns: Address the ethical concerns that arise from clickbait practices, such as misleading headlines, sensationalism, and the potential spread of misinformation.

Audience Perception and Trust

Trust in Media: Examine the impact of clickbait on public trust in media. Consistent exposure to sensationalized or misleading content can erode audience trust, leading to skepticism about the credibility of news sources.

Audience Fragmentation: Discuss how clickbait contributes to audience fragmentation, with readers gravitating towards niche sites that reinforce their views, often at the expense of exposure to a diversity of perspectives.

Adaptations and Innovations in Journalism

Emergence of Fact-Checking and Verification Platforms: Highlight the rise of fact-checking platforms and initiatives aimed at combating misinformation and restoring trust in journalism.

Innovative Storytelling Techniques: Explore how some media outlets are using innovative storytelling techniques to engage audiences, combining clickbait-style headlines with in-depth, quality journalism.

Conclusion: The Future of Journalism in the Clickbait Era

Conclude by reflecting on the future of journalism in an age dominated by clickbait. This includes potential strategies for media outlets to balance the need for engagement with the commitment to journalistic excellence and the ongoing efforts to adapt to a rapidly evolving media landscape.

Effects On Journalistic Standards And Ethics

Compromising Journalistic Integrity

The rise of clickbait has posed significant challenges to journalistic integrity. In the race to attract clicks, some media outlets may prioritize sensational or provocative content over accuracy and depth. This trend risks undermining the core journalistic values of truthfulness, impartiality, and responsibility to the public.

The Shift in News Values

Traditional news values like significance, relevance, and accuracy can take a backseat in a clickbait-centric media environment. The emphasis often shifts to what is most sensational or what can generate the most immediate engagement, rather than what is most informative or relevant to public discourse.

Sensationalism and Misleading Headlines

A common practice in clickbait is the use of sensational or misleading headlines. These headlines may overpromise, oversimplify, or misrepresent the content, leading readers to expect something different from what the article actually delivers. This practice not only deceives the audience but can also contribute to the spread of misinformation.

Ethical Dilemmas in Story Selection

The prevalence of clickbait influences the types of stories that get coverage. Media outlets might favor light, entertaining stories or emotionally charged content over more important but less sensational news, leading to an imbalance in news reporting and a potential neglect of critical issues.

Impact on Public Trust

Persistent exposure to clickbait can erode public trust in media. When audiences consistently encounter exaggerated or sensational content, their confidence in the media's ability to provide accurate and reliable information diminishes. This erosion of trust is a significant concern for the credibility and sustainability of news organizations.

Balancing Engagement with Ethical Reporting

Media outlets face the challenge of balancing the need for engagement (and the resulting revenue) with the principles of ethical journalism. This balance is crucial for maintaining a healthy, informed public discourse. Outlets must navigate the pressures of a digital economy while upholding their duty to provide accurate, fair, and meaningful content.

Conclusion

The impact of clickbait on journalistic standards and ethics is a pressing issue in the modern media landscape. As media outlets adapt to the digital age, finding ways to engage audiences without compromising journalistic integrity remains a critical challenge. The future of journalism may depend on developing sustainable models that can harmonize the demands of a digital audience with the fundamental principles of ethical reporting.

The Balance Between Traffic And Credibility

In the digital age, media outlets are constantly grappling with the challenge of balancing the need for web traffic with the imperative of maintaining credibility. This delicate equilibrium is at the heart of modern journalism's struggle in an era dominated by clickbait and fast-paced online consumption.

The Drive for Digital Traffic

Economic Pressures: Many media organizations operate under models where traffic directly correlates with revenue, primarily through advertising. This creates an incentive to produce content that is more likely to attract clicks and, consequently, more views and higher advertising income.

Visibility in the Digital Space: In the crowded digital landscape, getting noticed often requires headlines and content that are immediately engaging. This necessity can push outlets towards clickbait-style tactics to stand out and capture fleeting online attention spans.

Upholding Journalistic Credibility

Trust as a Foundation: Credibility and trust are the bedrock of any reputable media organization. Upholding journalistic standards — accuracy, impartiality, and responsible reporting — is crucial in maintaining the trust of the audience.

Long-term Impact on Reputation: While sensationalized content might boost short-term traffic, it can erode a media outlet's reputation over time. An outlet known for prioritizing traffic over truth risks losing its most valuable asset — the trust of its readers.

Finding the Middle Ground

Innovative Engagement Strategies: Some media outlets are exploring innovative ways to engage readers without resorting to clickbait. This includes investing in quality storytelling, interactive content, and data journalism that attract readers based on the merit of the content rather than sensational headlines.

Reader Engagement beyond Clicks: Shifting the focus from mere click counts to deeper engagement metrics — such as time spent on page, return visits, and reader interaction — can encourage more substantial content strategies that balance traffic goals with credibility.

The Role of Audience Education

Fostering Media Literacy: Educating the audience about media consumption, the pitfalls of clickbait, and the importance of supporting credible journalism can play a significant role in shifting demand towards more trustworthy content.

Building a Loyal Audience Base: By consistently providing high-quality, reliable content, media outlets can cultivate a loyal audience that values credibility over sensationalism. This loyalty can translate into sustainable traffic and revenue in the long run.

Conclusion

Navigating the balance between traffic and credibility is one of the most significant challenges facing media organizations today. Success in this endeavor requires not only strategic content planning but also a commitment to the principles of ethical journalism. As the media landscape continues to evolve, this balance will remain a critical factor in shaping the future of news and information dissemination.

The Economic Incentives Behind Clickbait

The proliferation of clickbait in digital media is largely driven by underlying economic incentives. Understanding these incentives is key to comprehending why clickbait has become a staple in online content creation and distribution.

Advertising Revenue Model

Pay-Per-Click and Impressions: Most online media outlets rely heavily on advertising revenue, which is often generated on a pay-per-click or per-impression basis. Clickbait articles, with their high click-through rates, are particularly effective at driving traffic, thereby increasing potential ad revenue.

The More Clicks, The More Revenue: The direct correlation between the number of clicks and advertising revenue incentivizes content creators to produce headlines and articles that are more likely to be clicked, often at the expense of content quality or accuracy.

Competition for Attention in a Crowded Space

Attention Economy: In the vast landscape of the internet, the competition for user attention is fierce. Clickbait emerges as a strategy to cut through the noise and capture that attention, even if momentarily.

Viral Potential: Content that has the potential to go viral, a characteristic often associated with clickbait, can exponentially increase an outlet's visibility and revenue potential.

The Role of Social Media

Amplification Through Sharing: Social media platforms amplify the reach of clickbait content. Articles with sensational or provocative headlines are more likely to be shared, leading to increased traffic and, by extension, more ad revenue.

Algorithmic Advantages: As social media algorithms often prioritize content that generates engagement, clickbait headlines that provoke reactions (likes, shares, comments) are more likely to be seen by a larger audience.

Cost-Effectiveness of Clickbait Production

Low Production Costs: Clickbait articles can be relatively inexpensive to produce, especially compared to in-depth investigative journalism. This low-cost, high-return model is economically attractive to content producers operating under budget constraints.

Rapid Content Turnaround: The quick turnaround time for producing clickbait content allows for a higher volume of articles, further driving web traffic and ad revenue.

Audience Metrics and Valuation

Metrics of Success: In the digital media industry, success is often measured by traffic metrics — clicks, page views, and time spent on site. Clickbait directly contributes to these metrics, making it a valuable tool in the eyes of advertisers and investors.

Valuation and Investment: For media companies, high traffic numbers and engagement rates can lead to higher valuations and increased investment, further reinforcing the reliance on clickbait strategies.

Conclusion

The economic incentives behind clickbait highlight a fundamental challenge in digital media — balancing the drive for revenue with the commitment to quality content and journalistic integrity. As the media landscape evolves, finding sustainable models that align economic success with ethical content creation remains a critical pursuit for the industry.

Chapter 7: Ethical And Legal Considerations

Introduction: Ethics and Law in the Age of Clickbait

This chapter addresses the ethical dilemmas and legal challenges posed by clickbait in digital media. It explores how the pursuit of clicks can sometimes lead to questionable practices, examining the implications for both media producers and consumers.

Ethical Challenges in Clickbait Practices

Misleading Content: Discuss the ethical concerns associated with headlines that promise more than the content delivers or sensationalize facts. This practice can mislead readers and erode trust in media sources.

Manipulation of Emotions: Delve into the ethics of manipulating readers' emotions for clicks, and the potential harm this can cause, such as spreading fear or misinformation.

Balancing Traffic and Truth: Explore the ethical dilemma faced by media outlets in balancing the pursuit of web traffic with the responsibility to provide accurate and reliable information.

Legal Implications and Challenges

False Advertising and Consumer Protection Laws: Examine how clickbait practices can sometimes border on false advertising, leading to potential legal issues under consumer protection laws.

Defamation and Privacy Concerns: Discuss the legal risks associated with clickbait that may infringe on individuals' privacy rights or lead to defamation, especially in the case of sensationalized or unverified content.

Intellectual Property Issues: Consider the legal aspects of using images, videos, and other media in clickbait content, which can sometimes lead to copyright infringement.

The Role of Regulation and Self-Regulation

Media Regulation Policies: Assess the role of government regulations in curbing unethical clickbait practices, and the challenges in implementing effective regulatory frameworks that balance free speech and responsible journalism.

Industry Self-Regulation: Explore the efforts within the media industry to self-regulate, including the adoption of ethical guidelines, fact-checking initiatives, and transparency measures to build trust with audiences.

The Impact on Public Discourse and Democracy

Influence on Public Opinion: Reflect on how clickbait, particularly when spreading misinformation, can influence public opinion and political discourse, potentially impacting democratic processes.

Responsibility Towards Public Discourse: Discuss the media's responsibility in fostering informed and healthy public discourse, and the role of clickbait in fulfilling or hindering this responsibility.

Conclusion: Navigating the Ethical Landscape

Conclude by contemplating the future of ethical considerations in digital media. Emphasize the importance of finding a balance that allows for both engaging content and ethical journalistic practices, and the ongoing need for dialogue and action among media producers, regulators, and consumers in shaping this balance.

The Line Between Marketing And Misinformation

The Blurred Boundaries in Digital Media

Introduction to the Dilemma: In the digital media landscape, the line between marketing content (designed to attract and engage audiences) and misinformation (which can mislead and deceive) is often blurred. This section sets the stage for understanding the complexities involved in differentiating between effective marketing strategies and the propagation of misinformation.

Characteristics of Marketing and Misinformation

Marketing Techniques: Marketing in digital media typically involves strategies aimed at capturing attention, building brand awareness, and driving consumer engagement. This includes the use of catchy headlines, persuasive language, and compelling visuals, all intended to draw in the audience.

Nature of Misinformation: Misinformation, on the other hand, involves the dissemination of false or misleading information. In the context of clickbait, it can manifest as exaggerated claims, sensationalized stories, or decontextualized facts that create a false impression.

Ethical Marketing vs. Misinformation

Ethical Considerations in Marketing: Ethical marketing respects the intelligence and autonomy of the audience. It focuses on providing truthful and relevant information, even while employing persuasive techniques.

Misinformation as Unethical Practice: Misinformation, by its nature, is unethical as it deceives the audience, often for financial gain, political influence, or other hidden agendas. It can lead to misinformed decisions, eroded trust, and harm to public discourse.

The Challenge of Identifying Misinformation

Subtlety of Misinformation: In many cases, misinformation is not overtly false but rather subtly misleading. It may involve truth stretched to serve a particular narrative or important details omitted to change the story's implication.

Difficulty in Distinguishing: For the average consumer, distinguishing between clever marketing and misinformation can be challenging, especially when the content is designed to appeal to emotions or preconceived notions.

The Role of Media Literacy

Educating Consumers: Strengthening media literacy is essential in empowering consumers to differentiate between marketing and misinformation. This includes understanding how to critically evaluate sources, check facts, and recognize biases.

Responsibility of Content Creators: Content creators and marketers also bear responsibility for ensuring their techniques do not cross into the realm of misinformation. Maintaining transparency and adhering to ethical standards is key to preserving credibility.

Legal and Regulatory Perspectives

Regulations on Misinformation and Advertising: Discuss the existing legal frameworks and regulations that address false advertising and misinformation, and their role in mitigating deceptive practices.

Challenges in Enforcement: Highlight the challenges in enforcing these regulations, especially in the rapidly evolving and borderless digital media space.

Conclusion: Striving for Balance

The chapter concludes with a call for a balanced approach where marketing in digital media is conducted responsibly and ethically, with a conscious effort to avoid veering into misinformation. This balance is crucial for maintaining a healthy, informed, and trustworthy digital ecosystem.

Legal Cases And Controversies Involving Clickbait

Introduction to Legal Challenges in Clickbait

The chapter opens by framing the legal landscape surrounding clickbait, highlighting how its use has led to various legal controversies and cases. These legal issues not only underscore the potential risks associated with clickbait but also illustrate the evolving nature of law in the digital age.

Notable Legal Cases Involving Clickbait

Misleading Advertising: Discuss cases where media outlets or companies faced legal action due to clickbait that was deemed misleading or false advertising. These cases often hinge on whether the clickbait content could reasonably deceive an average consumer, leading to misconceptions about a product or service.

Defamation and Libel: Explore instances where clickbait headlines or content led to defamation lawsuits. These cases typically involve sensationalized or misleading headlines that harm an individual's or organization's reputation.

Privacy Violations: Highlight legal controversies where clickbait content has infringed on individuals' privacy rights, such as using someone's image without consent or sharing private information without authorization.

Regulatory Responses to Clickbait

Consumer Protection Laws: Examine how consumer protection laws have been applied to cases of clickbait, particularly in instances where it crosses into deceptive advertising.

Regulatory Bodies and Clickbait: Discuss the role of regulatory bodies, like the Federal Trade Commission (FTC) in the United States, in setting guidelines and taking action against misleading digital content practices.

The Challenges of Legal Enforcement

Jurisdictional Issues: Address the challenges of enforcing legal actions in the digital realm, where content can cross national borders and fall under multiple jurisdictions.

Rapid Evolution of Digital Media: Consider the difficulties in applying existing laws to the fast-evolving nature of digital media and online content strategies, including clickbait.

The Role of Self-Regulation and Industry Standards

Media Self-Regulation: Explore how the media industry has responded to the legal and ethical challenges of clickbait through self-regulation, including the adoption of codes of conduct and ethical guidelines.

The Impact of Public Outcry and Advocacy: Reflect on how public outcry and advocacy groups have influenced the approach of media outlets and platforms to clickbait, leading to more responsible practices.

Conclusion: Navigating the Legal Terrain

Conclude by underscoring the importance of ongoing vigilance and adaptation in legal and regulatory frameworks to keep pace with the changing landscape of digital media. Emphasize the need for a collaborative effort between legal bodies, the media industry, and the public to ensure that clickbait practices do not infringe on legal rights or ethical standards.

Ethical Dilemmas For Content Creators

Introduction to Ethical Challenges in Content Creation

The chapter begins by setting the context for the ethical dilemmas faced by content creators in the digital age, particularly in relation to the use of clickbait. It emphasizes the fine line between engaging audiences and misleading them, a line that content creators must navigate daily.

The Temptation of Clickbait

Engagement vs. Misinformation: Discuss the temptation to use sensationalized or misleading headlines to drive traffic and engagement, versus the responsibility to provide accurate and reliable information.

Short-term Gains vs. Long-term Credibility: Explore the dilemma between achieving short-term gains in traffic and ad revenue through clickbait and maintaining long-term credibility and trust with the audience.

Balancing Creativity with Responsibility

Creative Freedom: Address the challenge of exercising creative freedom in content creation while ensuring that this creativity does not morph into deception or sensationalism.

Responsibility to the Audience: Delve into the moral responsibility of content creators to respect their audience, avoiding tactics that exploit cognitive biases or mislead for the sake of clicks.

The Pressure of Economic Incentives

Revenue-driven Strategies: Examine how the pressure to generate revenue, particularly in ad-based business models, can lead to ethical dilemmas in content creation.

Balancing Economic Needs and Ethical Standards: Discuss strategies for balancing the economic needs of a media outlet or platform with adherence to ethical standards in content creation.

Navigating the Social Impact

Influence on Public Discourse: Consider the impact that clickbait can have on public discourse and opinion, especially when it involves sensationalizing serious issues or spreading misinformation.

Social Responsibility: Reflect on the social responsibility of content creators to contribute positively to the information ecosystem, avoiding content that can misinform or harm public understanding.

Ethical Guidelines and Best Practices

Developing Ethical Guidelines: Discuss the importance of establishing ethical guidelines for content creation, including clear policies on clickbait and misinformation.

Best Practices for Ethical Content Creation: Provide insights into best practices that content creators can adopt to ensure their work remains engaging yet truthful and responsible.

Conclusion: The Path Forward for Ethical Content Creation

Conclude by reinforcing the importance of ethical considerations in content creation. Highlight the role of content creators in shaping an informed, healthy digital media landscape and the need for continuous reflection and adaptation to uphold ethical standards in a rapidly evolving digital world.

Chapter 8: Fighting Back Against Clickbait

Introduction: The Push Against Clickbait

This chapter delves into the various strategies and efforts being employed to combat the prevalence of clickbait. It explores the roles of individual consumers, content creators, social media platforms, and regulatory bodies in addressing the challenges posed by clickbait.

Empowering Consumers: Media Literacy and Awareness

Enhancing Media Literacy: Discuss the importance of educating internet users on identifying clickbait, understanding its impact, and making informed choices about what to click and share.

Critical Thinking Skills: Emphasize the need for developing critical thinking skills to evaluate the credibility of online content and to discern between sensationalized and genuine news.

Content Creators' Responsibility

Adopting Ethical Practices: Encourage content creators to adopt more ethical practices in content production, focusing on accuracy and substance over sensationalism.

Transparency with Audiences: Urge creators to be transparent about their content, including the use of clear labeling when content is sponsored or contains advertising.

Social Media Platforms' Role

Algorithm Adjustments: Examine how social media platforms are adjusting their algorithms to reduce the visibility of clickbait and prioritize quality content.

Fact-Checking and Content Moderation: Discuss the implementation of fact-checking tools and content moderation strategies by platforms to identify and limit the spread of misleading or sensationalized content.

Regulatory Measures and Policies

Government and Policy Interventions: Explore the role of government regulations and policies in curbing clickbait, including potential legislation and guidelines for digital content.

International Cooperation: Highlight the need for international cooperation in addressing clickbait, considering the global nature of the internet and digital media.

Industry Initiatives and Self-Regulation

Media Industry Standards: Consider the development of industry-wide standards and codes of conduct that discourage clickbait and promote ethical journalism.

Self-Regulation and Peer Review: Encourage media outlets and platforms to adopt self-regulatory measures and peer review mechanisms to maintain content integrity.

The Future of Content in the Digital Age

Innovations in Content Presentation: Look into innovative ways of presenting content that can engage audiences without resorting to clickbait tactics.

Building Trust and Credibility: Discuss the importance of building and maintaining trust with audiences as a long-term strategy against the culture of clickbait.

Conclusion: A Collective Effort Against Clickbait

Conclude with a call to action, emphasizing that fighting clickbait requires a collective effort from all stakeholders in the digital ecosystem. Highlight the importance of continued vigilance, innovation, and collaboration in creating a more informed and authentic online media environment.

Tools And Techniques For Identifying Clickbait

Critical Evaluation of Headlines

Sensationalism and Exaggeration: Teach readers to be wary of headlines that use sensational language or make exaggerated claims. Phrases like "You won't believe…" or "This will shock you…" are common markers of clickbait.

Headline-Content Consistency: Encourage readers to assess whether the headline accurately reflects the content of the article. A disconnect between the two is a common trait of clickbait.

Analyzing the Source

Reputable Sources: Emphasize the importance of considering the credibility of the source. Trusted and reputable publications are less likely to rely on clickbait tactics.

Author Credentials: Checking the author's credentials can provide insights into the reliability of the content. Established journalists and experts in the field are less likely to produce clickbait.

Understanding Clickbait Structures

Listicles and Emotional Appeals: Make readers aware of common clickbait formats, such as listicles (e.g., "Top 10 ways..."), and content that plays heavily on emotions.

Curiosity Gap Techniques: Educate about the curiosity gap technique, where the headline poses a question or makes a partial revelation, prompting readers to click for more information.

Digital Literacy and Media Education

Media Literacy Programs: Advocate for media literacy education that includes training on identifying and understanding clickbait.

Online Resources and Guides: Direct readers to online resources, guides, and workshops that offer more comprehensive training on discerning clickbait.

Fact-Checking and Verification Tools

Fact-Checking Websites: Encourage the use of fact-checking websites to verify the authenticity of sensational news or claims.

Browser Extensions: Introduce browser extensions designed to flag or block clickbait and misleading content.

Technical Tools and AI

AI-Based Detection Tools: Discuss emerging AI-based tools and algorithms that are being developed to automatically detect and flag clickbait content.

Analytical Tools for Engagement Patterns: Mention tools that analyze engagement patterns and metadata to identify potential clickbait articles.

Encouraging Skepticism and Verification

Healthy Skepticism: Foster a mindset of healthy skepticism where readers take a moment to critically think about a headline before clicking or sharing.

Verification Habits: Promote the habit of verifying sensational or surprising information through multiple sources before accepting it as true.

Conclusion: Building a Clickbait-Resilient Mindset

Conclude by reinforcing the idea that identifying clickbait requires a combination of critical thinking, media literacy, and the judicious use of available tools and resources. Empowering readers to recognize and resist clickbait is a crucial step towards fostering a more informed and discerning online community.

Role Of Media Literacy In Combating Clickbait

Understanding Media Literacy

Definition and Importance: Begin by defining media literacy as the ability to access, analyze, evaluate, create, and act using all forms of communication. Explain its importance in enabling individuals to critically understand and interact with media, especially in an age dominated by digital content.

Media Literacy as a Tool Against Clickbait

Critical Analysis of Content: Emphasize how media literacy equips individuals with the skills to critically analyze the content they encounter. This includes distinguishing between credible journalism and clickbait, understanding the motives behind different types of content, and recognizing bias and sensationalism.

Evaluating Sources: Media literacy involves assessing the credibility of sources. Educated readers are more likely to question the authenticity of a source and check its reliability, which is crucial in the age of clickbait and misinformation.

Developing Media Literacy Skills

Educational Programs: Discuss the role of educational programs in schools and communities that focus on developing critical thinking and media analysis skills.

Self-Education: Encourage self-education practices, such as attending workshops, online courses, or reading books and articles on media literacy.

Media Literacy in Digital Spaces

Navigating Online Platforms: Detail how media literacy helps in navigating digital platforms where clickbait is prevalent. This includes understanding how algorithms work, the nature of targeted advertising, and the tactics used by clickbait creators.

Social Media Responsibility: Talk about the responsible use of social media, including being mindful of what content is shared and engaging in constructive online discussions.

Combating Misinformation and Sensationalism

Fact-Checking and Verification: Stress the importance of fact-checking and verification as part of media literacy. This includes using reputable fact-checking sites and learning how to cross-check information.

Understanding Clickbait Strategies: Highlight how media literacy helps in understanding and recognizing the strategies used in clickbait, such as emotional manipulation and the curiosity gap.

Encouraging Proactive Consumer Behavior

Active Engagement: Discuss how media literacy encourages consumers to be proactive rather than passive receivers of information. This includes questioning content, seeking diverse perspectives, and contributing to media literacy awareness.

Reporting and Feedback: Explain how media-literate individuals can play a role in combating clickbait by reporting misleading content and providing feedback to platforms and content creators.

Conclusion: A Collective Responsibility

Conclude by emphasizing that combating clickbait is a collective responsibility. Media literacy is not just about individual empowerment but also about fostering a more informed, responsible, and discerning society that values truth and integrity in media content.

Initiatives By Platforms And Governments

Social Media Platforms' Efforts

Algorithm Adjustments: Many social media platforms have modified their algorithms to de-prioritize clickbait. These adjustments aim to reduce the visibility of sensationalist, misleading, or superficial content in favor of more authentic and reliable material.

Fact-Checking Partnerships: Platforms like Facebook and Twitter have partnered with third-party fact-checkers to identify and label misinformation and clickbait, offering corrections and additional context to users.

User Education: Some platforms have launched initiatives to educate users about misinformation and clickbait, including tips on how to spot and report such content.

Content Moderation Policies: Updating content moderation policies to specifically address clickbait and implementing stricter consequences for repeatedly posting misleading content.

Governmental and Regulatory Actions

Legislation Against Misinformation: Certain governments have introduced or are considering legislation that targets the spread of misinformation online, which includes punitive measures for platforms that fail to adequately address the issue.

Consumer Protection Laws: Applying consumer protection laws to digital content, ensuring that advertising and headlines do not mislead or deceive consumers.

Public Awareness Campaigns: Governments, often in collaboration with non-profit organizations, have launched public awareness campaigns to educate citizens about media literacy, including how to recognize and resist clickbait.

Cross-Industry Collaborations

Media Standards and Guidelines: Efforts to develop industry-wide standards and ethical guidelines that discourage clickbait practices and promote responsible journalism.

Collaborative Research: Joint research initiatives between academia, industry, and governments to study the effects of clickbait and develop effective counter-strategies.

Technological Innovations

Development of Detection Tools: Investment in the development of AI and machine learning tools that can automatically detect clickbait and assess the reliability of content.

Enhanced User Control: Introducing features that give users more control over what they see in their feeds, such as options to flag or hide clickbait content.

Challenges and Considerations

Balancing Free Speech: Address the challenge of balancing the reduction of clickbait with the protection of free speech and preventing censorship.

Global Coordination: Highlight the need for global coordination and cooperation, given the borderless nature of the internet and digital media.

Conclusion: A Multifaceted Approach

Conclude by emphasizing that reducing the prevalence of clickbait requires a multifaceted approach involving platforms, governments, industry bodies, and users. These initiatives, while promising, must continuously evolve to effectively counter sophisticated and ever-changing clickbait tactics in the digital landscape.

Chapter 9: The Future Of Clickbait

Introduction: The Evolving Landscape of Digital Content

This chapter opens with a reflection on the dynamic nature of digital media and the ever-evolving landscape of clickbait. It sets the stage for exploring potential future trends, challenges, and the evolving relationship between clickbait and digital content consumption.

Advancements in Technology and Clickbait

AI and Machine Learning: Discuss how advancements in artificial intelligence and machine learning could lead to more sophisticated clickbait strategies, capable of personalizing content to individual users' preferences and behaviors.

Augmented Reality and Virtual Reality: Explore the potential for clickbait to extend into emerging digital realms like augmented reality (AR) and virtual reality (VR), creating new dimensions of engagement and challenges.

Changing User Behaviors and Expectations

Increasing Savviness of Users: Acknowledge that as users become more internet-savvy, their ability to recognize and ignore clickbait may increase, potentially leading to a decline in its effectiveness.

Demand for Authenticity: Project how growing user demand for authenticity and transparency in digital content could shape the evolution of clickbait, possibly steering content creators towards more ethical practices.

The Role of Social Media Platforms

Platform Policies and Regulations: Delve into how social media platforms might continue to refine their policies and algorithms to reduce the prevalence of clickbait, in response to user feedback and regulatory pressures.

Emergence of New Platforms: Consider the impact of new social media platforms and how their unique features and user bases could influence clickbait trends.

Regulatory and Ethical Considerations

Global Regulations: Discuss the potential for more stringent global regulations aimed at curbing misleading digital content, including clickbait, and how this might shape its future.

Ethical Shifts in Content Creation: Contemplate a future where there's a stronger ethical shift in content creation, with an emphasis on responsible journalism and credible information dissemination.

Innovations in Counter-Clickbait Strategies

Development of Anti-Clickbait Tools: Predict advancements in tools and technologies designed to help users and platforms identify and filter out clickbait content.

Educational Initiatives: Foresee a rise in media literacy initiatives focusing on equipping users with skills to critically evaluate and resist clickbait content.

Conclusion: The Changing Face of Clickbait

Conclude by reflecting on the adaptability of clickbait and its likely persistence in the digital landscape, albeit in evolving forms. Emphasize that the future of clickbait will be shaped by a complex interplay of technological advancements, user behavior, platform policies, and regulatory frameworks. The conclusion should leave readers with an understanding that while clickbait may change, the need for critical engagement with digital content remains constant.

Emerging Trends And Technologies

AI-Generated Content

Rise of AI in Content Creation: Discuss how artificial intelligence is increasingly being used to generate content, including articles, social media posts, and even entire websites. This technology can produce vast amounts of content quickly, potentially leading to a surge in AI-generated clickbait.

Personalization at Scale: Explore how AI can tailor clickbait to individual users by analyzing their online behavior, preferences, and engagement patterns, leading to highly personalized and potentially more effective clickbait.

Deepfakes and Synthetic Media

The Deepfake Phenomenon: Examine the implications of deepfake technology, which can create highly realistic but entirely fabricated audiovisual content. This could take clickbait to a new level of deception, with fake but convincing videos or audio clips used to attract clicks.

Challenges in Authenticity: Discuss the challenges deepfakes pose in distinguishing between real and synthetic media, and the potential for their use in sophisticated clickbait strategies.

Interactive and Immersive Content

Engagement through Interactivity: Predict the rise of interactive clickbait, where users are drawn into engaging with content through quizzes, polls, and interactive storytelling. This could lead to more nuanced and engaging forms of clickbait.

Virtual and Augmented Reality: Consider how VR and AR technologies could be used to create immersive clickbait experiences, offering users seemingly tangible but ultimately sensationalized or misleading content.

Blockchain and Content Verification

Blockchain for Verification: Discuss how blockchain technology could be used to verify the authenticity of content, potentially countering the spread of misleading clickbait. This could involve certifying sources or tracking content modifications.

Decentralization of Content: Explore the potential for decentralized content platforms, powered by blockchain, to offer alternatives to traditional media and social platforms where clickbait thrives.

The Evolution of Social Media Algorithms

Smarter Algorithms: Consider how future developments in social media algorithms could more effectively identify and demote clickbait content, based on user engagement patterns and feedback.

Ethical AI Use in Content Curation: Delve into the ethical use of AI in curating content feeds, balancing user engagement with the promotion of credible and informative content.

Ethical AI and the Future of Content Creation

Setting Ethical Standards for AI: Discuss the importance of setting ethical standards for AI in content creation, ensuring that these technologies are used responsibly and do not contribute to the spread of clickbait.

AI as a Tool for Detecting Clickbait: Explore how AI can also be used to detect and flag clickbait content, assisting platforms and users in identifying misleading headlines and articles.

Conclusion: Navigating a Tech-Driven Future

Conclude by acknowledging the double-edged nature of emerging technologies in the context of clickbait. While they present new challenges in content authenticity and integrity, they also offer innovative tools for combating misleading content. The future landscape of clickbait will likely be shaped by how effectively these technologies are harnessed, regulated, and ethically integrated into digital media.

Predictions For The Evolution Of Clickbait

Increased Sophistication in Targeting and Personalization

Advanced Data Analytics: As data analytics become more sophisticated, expect clickbait strategies to increasingly tailor content to individual user preferences, browsing history, and behavior, making them more effective and harder to resist.

Micro-targeting: Future clickbait might use micro-targeting techniques to appeal to very specific interests or demographics, leveraging detailed user data to create highly personalized clickbait.

Integration with Emerging Technologies

AI and Machine Learning: Anticipate that AI and machine learning algorithms will be employed to not only create but also optimize clickbait content in real-time, adjusting headlines and content based on user engagement metrics.

Augmented and Virtual Reality: As AR and VR technologies mature, clickbait strategies might involve immersive experiences, drawing users into interactive scenarios that blur the lines between reality and sensationalized content.

Shift in Content Formats and Platforms

Beyond Text and Images: Expect clickbait to evolve beyond traditional text and image formats. This could include interactive videos, gamified content, or even AI-generated music and podcasts designed to hook users.

New Platforms and Mediums: With the continual emergence of new social media platforms and digital mediums, clickbait strategies will likely adapt to these new environments, exploiting platform-specific features and user behaviors.

Ethical and Subtle Clickbait

'Ethical' Clickbait: In response to growing awareness and backlash against deceptive clickbait, there might be a rise in 'ethical clickbait' – content that is still designed to be highly engaging and clickable but is more transparent and accurate in its representation.

Subtlety and Nuance: Future clickbait might become more subtle and nuanced, moving away from overt sensationalism to more cleverly crafted headlines and content that still pique curiosity but are less obviously clickbait.

Reactive and Adaptive Content

Responsive Content: Clickbait strategies could become more reactive to current events, social trends, and user-generated content, quickly adapting and morphing to maintain relevance and engagement.

User-Generated Clickbait: The rise of user-generated content platforms might see an increase in clickbait created not by organizations or businesses but by individuals, as part of personal branding or as a means to gain followers and visibility.

Legal and Regulatory Influences

Compliance with Regulations: As governments and regulatory bodies impose stricter guidelines on online content, clickbait strategies may evolve to comply with these regulations while still striving to capture user attention effectively.

Self-Regulation by Platforms: Anticipate that social media platforms and content hosts will continue to refine their policies and algorithms to limit traditional clickbait, pushing creators to innovate new methods that align with platform standards.

Conclusion: A Dynamic Future for Clickbait

Conclude by highlighting that the future of clickbait is dynamic and uncertain, shaped by technological advances, user behavior, regulatory environments, and ethical considerations. While the core objective of attracting user attention will remain, the strategies employed will likely become more refined, personalized, and integrated with emerging digital trends.

Potential Impact Of Regulatory Changes

The Potential Impact of Regulatory Changes

Introduction: Regulation in the Digital Media Landscape

The chapter opens with an overview of the growing call for regulatory changes in the digital media landscape, particularly in response to the challenges posed by clickbait and misleading content. It sets the stage for exploring how potential regulatory shifts could impact the production and dissemination of clickbait.

Stricter Content Regulations

Impact on Content Creation: Discuss how stricter regulations aimed at curbing misleading or sensationalized content could lead to significant changes in how clickbait is created. Content creators might be required to adhere to higher standards of accuracy and transparency.

Reduction in Misleading Practices: Anticipate that tighter regulations could lead to a reduction in blatantly misleading or deceptive clickbait practices, as the legal and financial risks of non-compliance increase.

Enhanced Transparency and Disclosure Requirements

Mandatory Disclosures: Explore the potential requirement for clearer disclosures on sponsored content and advertising, making it harder for clickbait to masquerade as genuine editorial content.

User Awareness: Consider how increased transparency could lead to greater awareness among users about the nature of the content they are consuming, potentially reducing the effectiveness of clickbait tactics.

The Role of Fact-Checking and Verification

Mandated Fact-Checking: Discuss the possibility of regulations requiring media outlets to implement more rigorous fact-checking processes, especially for content that has the potential to go viral or significantly impact public opinion.

Collaboration with Independent Bodies: Contemplate regulations encouraging or requiring collaboration with independent fact-checking organizations to verify content before it is published or shared widely.

Impact on Social Media Platforms

Algorithmic Accountability: Delve into how regulations might demand greater transparency and accountability from social media platforms regarding their algorithms, particularly how they promote or demote content.

Responsibility for Content: Consider the implications of regulations that hold platforms more accountable for the content they host, possibly leading to more proactive measures against clickbait.

International Regulatory Challenges

Cross-Border Enforcement: Address the challenges in enforcing regulations in the digital realm, where content transcends national boundaries. Discuss the need for international cooperation and harmonization of regulatory standards.

Balancing Free Speech Concerns: Explore how regulatory changes must balance the need to curb misleading content with the protection of free speech, avoiding censorship or the suppression of legitimate expression.

Innovations in Response to Regulations

Adaptation of Clickbait Strategies: Predict how content creators might innovate new strategies to comply with regulations while still engaging audiences effectively.

Emergence of New Platforms: Speculate on the possibility of new platforms emerging that cater to different regulatory environments or offer alternative models for content sharing and monetization.

Conclusion: Shaping the Future of Digital Content

Conclude by reflecting on how regulatory changes could significantly shape the future of digital content. Emphasize that while regulations aim to mitigate the negative aspects of clickbait, they also open doors to more ethical and responsible media practices, potentially leading to a healthier digital information ecosystem.

Chapter 10: Beyond Clickbait

Introduction: Envisioning a Post-Clickbait Era

This chapter begins by acknowledging the pervasive nature of clickbait in the digital landscape while envisioning a future that moves beyond these tactics. It emphasizes the potential for a digital media environment that prioritizes quality, authenticity, and value over mere clicks.

The Shift to Quality and Substance

Valuing Depth Over Sensationalism: Discuss the growing trend among some media outlets and content creators to focus on in-depth, well-researched, and informative content as an alternative to clickbait.

Audience Demand for Authenticity: Explore how changing audience preferences, with an increasing demand for authenticity and reliability, are driving content creators to adopt more substantive approaches.

Innovative Content Strategies

Storytelling and Narrative Journalism: Highlight the resurgence of storytelling and narrative journalism as powerful tools for engaging audiences without resorting to clickbait tactics.

Interactive and Multimedia Content: Explore how the use of interactive elements, multimedia, and innovative formats can captivate audiences, offering immersive experiences that go beyond traditional clickbait models.

Leveraging Technology for Positive Engagement

AI and Personalization for Good: Discuss how AI and machine learning can be used to personalize content recommendations based on user interests and preferences, promoting content that is engaging yet valuable and relevant.

Emerging Technologies: Consider the role of emerging technologies like augmented reality (AR) and virtual reality (VR) in creating new, engaging content experiences that do not rely on misleading headlines or sensationalism.

The Role of Ethics and Responsibility

Promoting Ethical Standards: Emphasize the importance of ethical standards in content creation, including transparency, accuracy, and respect for the audience.

Corporate Social Responsibility: Explore how corporate social responsibility in digital media can influence practices that prioritize societal well-being over clicks and engagement metrics.

Building Trust with Audiences

Long-term Relationship Building: Discuss the importance of building long-term relationships with audiences based on trust, credibility, and consistent delivery of quality content.

Community Engagement and Feedback: Highlight the role of community engagement and user feedback in shaping content strategies that align with audience needs and expectations.

Educating the Next Generation

Media Literacy and Critical Thinking: Stress the need for continued focus on media literacy education, empowering future generations to discern quality content and resist clickbait.

Nurturing Responsible Digital Citizens: Encourage initiatives that nurture responsible digital citizenship, where individuals not only consume but also create and share content responsibly.

Conclusion: A Hopeful Outlook for Digital Media

Conclude by offering a hopeful outlook for the future of digital media. Paint a picture of a landscape where the lessons learned from the era of clickbait lead to more responsible, engaging, and enriching digital content. Highlight the potential for a media environment that balances the need for engagement with a commitment to quality and ethical standards, benefiting both creators and consumers alike.

Alternative Strategies For Engagement

Emphasizing Quality and Depth

In-depth Reporting and Analysis: Focus on producing well-researched, in-depth articles that provide comprehensive analysis and insights, rather than superficial overviews. This approach can build a reputation for reliability and authority, attracting a loyal audience.

Long-Form Content: Encourage the creation of long-form content such as detailed guides, extensive reports, and thought-provoking essays. Such content can establish expertise and keep readers engaged for longer periods.

Interactive and Multimedia Elements

Interactive Features: Utilize interactive elements like quizzes, polls, and interactive infographics to engage readers in a dynamic way. These features can provide a more engaging experience than traditional clickbait.

Utilizing Video and Audio: Incorporate multimedia elements like videos, podcasts, and webinars. These formats can be more engaging and shareable, offering a richer experience than text-based clickbait.

Personalized and Customized Content

User Personalization: Leverage data analytics to offer personalized content experiences. Tailoring content to individual user interests can increase engagement without resorting to sensationalism.

Customized Newsletters and Alerts: Provide customized newsletters or alerts based on users' preferences and past interactions, ensuring that they receive content that is relevant and interesting to them.

Storytelling and Human Interest

Narrative Storytelling: Harness the power of storytelling to captivate audiences. Stories with strong, relatable characters or intriguing plots can attract and retain attention effectively.

Human Interest Stories: Focus on human interest stories that resonate emotionally with readers. Such stories can be powerful in creating connections and engagement.

Community Building and Interaction

Engaging with Comments: Actively engage with readers in the comments section to foster a community around the content. This engagement can increase loyalty and return visits.

User-Generated Content: Encourage user-generated content such as guest posts, reader stories, and community discussions. This approach not only diversifies content but also builds a sense of community and belonging.

Educational and Value-Added Content

How-To Guides and Tutorials: Create practical, educational content like how-to guides, tutorials, and explainer videos. This type of content provides real value to readers and can establish the site as a go-to resource.

Webinars and Workshops: Offer webinars, online workshops, or courses that provide educational value, drawing in audiences seeking to learn and grow.

Leveraging Social Issues and Trends

Addressing Current Issues: Develop content that addresses current social issues, trends, or news, providing insightful commentary or analysis. This approach can attract readers interested in understanding the world around them.

Thought Leadership: Position the brand or key individuals as thought leaders by publishing insightful opinions or perspectives on industry trends, future predictions, or societal changes.

Conclusion: Diversifying Engagement Strategies

Conclude by emphasizing the importance of diversifying content strategies to engage audiences in meaningful ways. Highlight that while alternative strategies may require more effort and creativity, they offer sustainable engagement based on genuine interest and value, fostering a more loyal and informed audience base.

Success Stories Of Quality Content Over Clickbait

Introduction: Celebrating Quality in the Digital Space

The chapter opens with an acknowledgment of the challenges faced in the digital content landscape, dominated by clickbait tactics. It then shifts to celebrate success stories where quality content has triumphed over clickbait, illustrating the potential for substantive and meaningful content to attract and retain audiences.

Case Study 1: The New York Times' Digital Transformation

Embracing Depth and Quality: Explore how The New York Times successfully transitioned to digital by focusing on in-depth reporting and quality journalism, rather than succumbing to clickbait trends.

Subscription Model Success: Highlight the success of their subscription model, which proved that audiences are willing to pay for quality, reliable content, defying the clickbait-dominated free content model.

Case Study 2: The Guardian's Open Journalism

Community Engagement: Discuss The Guardian's approach of open journalism, which involves engaging readers in the news process, offering transparency, and focusing on stories with depth and impact.

Sustainable Revenue Model: Examine their unique revenue model based on reader contributions, rejecting the clickbait model and prioritizing journalistic integrity.

Case Study 3: Vox Media's Explainer Journalism

Innovative Content Formats: Delve into how Vox Media has carved a niche in explainer journalism, using innovative formats and comprehensive analysis to engage readers.

Building Brand Loyalty: Show how their commitment to explaining complex topics in an accessible way has built a loyal audience base, setting them apart in a sea of sensationalist content.

Case Study 4: BBC's Fact-Checking Services

Counteracting Misinformation: Highlight BBC's efforts in fact-checking and debunking misinformation, providing a valuable resource in an era of fake news.

Global Trust and Credibility: Discuss how these efforts have reinforced BBC's position as a trusted global news source, attracting audiences seeking factual accuracy over sensationalism.

Case Study 5: Podcasts and Long-Form Audio Content

The Rise of Podcasts: Analyze the growing popularity of podcasts and long-form audio content, which often delve into topics with depth and nuance, contrary to clickbait practices.

Engagement Through Storytelling: Focus on successful podcasts that have captivated audiences with compelling storytelling and in-depth analysis, creating engaged communities.

Case Study 6: Independent Bloggers and Creators

Niche Content Success: Share stories of independent bloggers and content creators who have built substantial followings by offering specialized, high-quality content in niche areas.

Community and Trust: Emphasize how these creators have fostered trust and community, succeeding without relying on clickbait tactics.

Conclusion: The Enduring Value of Quality

Conclude by affirming the enduring value of quality content in the digital age. These success stories serve as a testament to the fact that while clickbait may offer short-term engagement, in the long run, it is the depth, credibility, and value of content that truly resonates with and retains audiences.

The Future Of Responsible Content Creation

Introduction: Embracing Ethical Practices in the Digital Age

This chapter begins by acknowledging the pivotal moment the digital content industry is facing, with increasing awareness and demand for ethical and responsible content creation. It sets the stage for a forward-looking discussion on the future of content creation that prioritizes integrity and value.

The Rise of Ethical Content Standards

Development of Global Standards: Explore the potential for the development and adoption of global ethical standards for content creation, focusing on accuracy, transparency, and fairness.

Industry-Wide Accountability: Discuss how media companies, independent creators, and platforms might increasingly hold themselves and each other accountable to these standards.

Leveraging Technology for Ethical Purposes

AI and Ethical Content Moderation: Predict the role of advanced AI in aiding ethical content moderation, helping to identify and limit the spread of misleading or harmful content.

Blockchain for Transparency: Consider the potential use of blockchain technology in content creation for ensuring the authenticity and traceability of information.

Shifting Business Models

Beyond Click-Based Revenue: Examine the shift towards alternative revenue models that don't rely solely on clicks and views, such as subscription models, crowdfunding, and direct support from readers.

Value-Based Advertising: Discuss the emergence of advertising models that align with ethical content standards, where ads are placed in a context that values quality and relevance over sheer traffic.

The Role of Education and Media Literacy

Empowering Consumers: Highlight the ongoing need for media literacy education to empower consumers to recognize and value responsible content.

Training for Content Creators: Advocate for more training and resources for content creators to understand and implement ethical practices in their work.

Collaborative Efforts and Partnerships

Cross-Sector Collaborations: Foresee collaborations between media companies, tech firms, non-profits, and educational institutions to promote responsible content creation and consumption.

Community-Driven Content: Predict the rise of community-driven content initiatives, where audience feedback and participation play a key role in shaping ethical content practices.

Innovations in Content Creation and Distribution

New Platforms and Tools: Speculate on the development of new platforms and tools that prioritize and promote ethical content, offering alternatives to traditional social media and content channels.

Diverse and Inclusive Content: Emphasize the importance of diversity and inclusivity in content creation, reflecting a broad spectrum of perspectives and experiences.

Conclusion: A Hopeful Outlook for Digital Content

Conclude by painting an optimistic picture of the future of content creation, one where integrity, responsibility, and audience trust are paramount. Stress that while challenges remain, the collective efforts of creators, platforms, and consumers can lead to a more ethical and enriching digital media landscape.

Conclusion

Charting a New Course in Digital Content

As we reach the conclusion of "A Study of ClickBait," it's clear that the journey through the intricate world of digital content has been both enlightening and complex. This book has traversed the diverse landscapes of clickbait – from its psychological underpinnings and economic motivations to its impact on journalism, media ethics, and the evolving dynamics in digital content consumption. Now, it's time to reflect on the key insights gleaned and contemplate the path forward in the ever-changing realm of digital media.

Summarizing The Key Findings And Insights

The Nature and Impact of Clickbait

Understanding Clickbait: We've delved into the essence of clickbait, uncovering its tactics of sensational headlines and emotionally charged content, designed to capture immediate attention and clicks.

Psychological Appeal: The book highlighted how clickbait effectively exploits psychological triggers such as curiosity, fear, and excitement, revealing why even the savviest users sometimes find themselves clicking on these enticing headlines.

The Digital Media Landscape

Economic Drivers: A key insight is the strong economic incentive behind clickbait, driven by an ad-based revenue model where clicks directly translate to income.

Impact on Journalism and Ethics: We observed the profound impact of clickbait on journalistic standards and media ethics, often leading to a compromise in content quality and reliability.

The Role of Technology and Social Media

Algorithms' Role: The book shed light on how social media algorithms often inadvertently favor clickbait by prioritizing content that engages users, thereby amplifying its reach.

Technological Advancements: The evolving role of AI and machine learning in both creating and combating clickbait was a significant focus, indicating a double-edged sword in technological progression.

Combating Clickbait

Media Literacy and Critical Thinking: One of the most crucial insights is the role of media literacy and critical thinking in combating clickbait, empowering readers to discern and choose quality content over sensationalism.

Platform and Regulatory Initiatives: We explored various initiatives by platforms and governments to curb clickbait, from algorithm adjustments to legal regulations.

The Future of Content Creation

Emerging Trends: Looking ahead, the book anticipated trends such as ethical content creation, innovative storytelling, and the use of immersive technologies, painting a hopeful picture of a more informed and authentic digital media environment.

The Balance of Engagement and Ethics: A recurring theme was the need for balancing audience engagement with ethical content practices, ensuring the integrity and sustainability of digital media.

A Call for Continued Evolution

In conclusion, "A Study of ClickBait" calls for a continued evolution in the digital media landscape. It advocates for a future where quality, ethics, and audience value take precedence over the transient allure of clickbait. As technology, user behavior, and media practices evolve, this book serves as a reminder and a guide for creators, consumers, and regulators to foster a responsible and enriching digital content ecosystem.

Personal Reflections On The Study Of Clickbait

As the author of "A Study of ClickBait," I find myself deeply immersed in the complex interplay of technology, psychology, and media that constitutes the world of clickbait. This journey has been enlightening, revealing not just the mechanics of clickbait, but also its broader implications for society and the way we consume information.

The Ubiquity and Influence of Clickbait

One of the most striking revelations has been the sheer ubiquity of clickbait and its profound influence on our daily online interactions. It's everywhere, shaping not only what we read and watch but also how we perceive the world around us. The realization of its omnipresence and impact has been both startling and sobering.

The Psychological Hook

Delving into the psychological aspects of clickbait was particularly fascinating. Understanding how human nature – our curiosities, fears, and desires – can be so effectively manipulated by headlines and content was a reminder of both the power and responsibility that comes with content creation. It underscored the fine line between engaging an audience and exploiting our innate tendencies.

Ethical and Moral Implications

Exploring the ethical dimensions of clickbait has been one of the more challenging aspects of this study. It raised important questions about the moral responsibilities of content creators and platforms. This inquiry into the ethical implications has been a call to action, highlighting the need for greater accountability in the digital media landscape.

The Role of Technology

The intersection of clickbait with emerging technologies like AI and machine learning was another key area of exploration. It was intriguing to see how these technologies can be a double-edged sword – capable of both exacerbating and alleviating the challenges of clickbait. This duality presents a complex but crucial frontier for future development and regulation.

Hope for the Future

Despite the challenges presented by clickbait, this study has also been a source of hope. Learning about the various initiatives to combat clickbait, the growing emphasis on media literacy, and the potential for more ethical content practices has been encouraging. It suggests a path forward where quality and integrity can coexist with digital innovation and audience engagement.

A Personal Journey of Learning

Finally, this journey through the world of clickbait has been a personal learning experience. It has not only broadened my understanding of digital media but also deepened my appreciation for responsible journalism and ethical content creation. As we move forward, it is my hope that this book will contribute to a more informed and discerning digital media environment for all.

Shaping a Responsible Digital Future

For Readers: Embrace Media Literacy and Critical Engagement

Be Discerning: Cultivate the habit of critically evaluating the content you consume. Look beyond headlines, question sensational claims, and check the credibility of sources.

Educate Yourself and Others: Invest time in enhancing your media literacy. Share your knowledge with others, especially in your immediate circles, to create a more informed community.

Engage Responsibly: When engaging with content online, do so responsibly. Avoid sharing unverified or sensationalized content, and use your interactions to promote meaningful discourse.

For Content Creators: Prioritize Integrity and Value

Commit to Ethical Standards: Uphold high standards of accuracy, fairness, and integrity in your content. Let your work be guided by a commitment to truth and value, rather than just clicks and views.

Innovate Creatively: Explore creative and innovative ways to engage your audience. Utilize storytelling, multimedia, and interactive content to captivate responsibly.

Foster Positive Impact: Aim for your content to not only attract but also enrich your audience. Strive to make a positive impact on public understanding and discourse.

For Platforms: Lead in Promoting Quality Content

Refine Algorithms for Quality: Adjust algorithms to prioritize and promote high-quality, informative content. Work towards a balance that values both engagement and credibility.

Support Ethical Practices: Implement and enforce policies that discourage clickbait and misleading content. Partner with fact-checkers and experts to maintain a high standard of content on your platform.

Empower Users: Provide tools and features that help users make informed choices about the content they consume and share. Encourage a culture of critical consumption and responsible sharing.

Conclusion: Collective Efforts for a Better Digital World

This call to action is a reminder that the fight against clickbait and the pursuit of a responsible digital media landscape is a collective effort. It requires the active participation of readers, the conscientiousness of creators, and the leadership of platforms. Together, we can shape a digital future that values authenticity, integrity, and meaningful engagement, fostering a healthier, more informed society.

Appendix

Additional Resources and Reading

1. **Books on Media Literacy and Digital Consumption**:

- Title: "Digital Literacy for Dummies" by Faithe Wempen
- Title: "The Filter Bubble: How the New Personalized Web Is Changing What We Read and How We Think" by Eli Pariser

2. **Articles and Research Papers**:

- "The Rise of Clickbait and the Changing Face of Online Journalism" - Harvard University Research Paper
- "Understanding the Psychology Behind Clickbait" - Journal of Digital Media Psychology

3. **Websites and Online Platforms for Fact-Checking**:

FactCheck.org: A nonpartisan, nonprofit consumer advocate for voters that monitors factual accuracy in U.S. politics.

4. **Online Courses on Content Creation and Digital Ethics**:

- "Ethics of Digital Content Creation" - Offered by Coursera
- "Media Literacy in the Digital Age" - Offered by edX

5. **Workshops and Webinars**:

- "Combating Misinformation Online" - Hosted by Media Literacy Now
- "Responsible Journalism in the Digital Age" - Hosted by the Poynter Institute

6. **Guides and Toolkits**:

- "A Guide to Recognizing and Avoiding Clickbait" - Published by the Digital Literacy Project
- "Toolkit for Responsible Digital Content Creation" - Developed by the Ethical Journalism Network

7. **Podcasts and Video Series**:

- "The Media Show" - A podcast exploring current issues in media and journalism
- "Crash Course Media Literacy" - A YouTube series that educates viewers on understanding media

8. **Organizations and Advocacy Groups**:

- The Center for Media Literacy: An organization dedicated to promoting media literacy education as a framework for accessing, analyzing, evaluating, creating, and participating with media content.
- The News Literacy Project: A nonpartisan national education nonprofit that provides programs and resources for educators and the public to teach, learn, and share the abilities needed to be smart, active consumers of news and information and equal and engaged participants in a democracy.

9. **Government and Regulatory Bodies' Publications**:

- Federal Communications Commission (FCC) reports on digital media and ethics
- European Commission papers on digital media regulations and policies

Further Tools and Platforms for Engagement and Learning

10. **Browser Extensions for Detecting Clickbait**:

- Clickbait Remover for YouTube: Modifies clickbait titles on YouTube to more straightforward descriptions.
- UnClickbait: An extension that replaces clickbait headlines with a summary of the article.

11. **Social Media Analytics Tools**:

- BuzzSumo: A tool for analyzing which content performs best on social media platforms.
- Hootsuite Insights: Provides insights into social media trends and audience behavior.

12. **Documentaries and Films on Media Influence**:

- "The Social Dilemma" - A documentary exploring the impact of social media on human behavior.
- "Trust Me" - A documentary examining the manipulation and misinformation in the age of the internet.

Associations and Networks Focused on Media Integrity

13. **International Federation of Journalists (IFJ)**: A global union federation of journalists' trade unions, committed to protecting and strengthening the rights and freedoms of journalists.
14. **World Association of News Publishers (WAN-IFRA)**: An organization that represents news publishers globally, promoting the rights of journalists and the free press.

Recommended Blogs and Online Forums

15. **Nieman Journalism Lab**: An attempt to help journalism figure out its future in an Internet age.
16. **MediaShift**: Provides insight and analysis at the intersection of media and technology.

Additional Reading and Reference Materials

17. **Government Reports on Digital Media Trends**: Comprehensive reports by various governments analyzing the impact of digital media on society and policy recommendations.
18. **Academic Journals on Media Studies**: Journals like the "Journal of Media Ethics" and "Digital Journalism" that offer scholarly insights into media trends and ethical considerations.

User Participation and Feedback Channels

19. **Feedback Platforms for Media Consumers**: Encourage readers to use platforms like Trustpilot or media outlets' own feedback channels to share their experiences and concerns about content quality.

Online Communities for Media Discussion: Platforms like Reddit or LinkedIn groups where media trends, ethics, and clickbait are regularly discussed and debated.

Glossary of Terms Related to Clickbait

Clickbait: Content, especially that of a sensational or provocative nature, whose main purpose is to attract attention and encourage visitors to click on a link to a particular web page.

Curiosity Gap: A marketing technique used to entice the audience, creating a gap between what the audience knows and what they want to know.

Algorithm: A process or set of rules followed by a computer in calculations or other problem-solving operations, especially in the context of software that determines which content is displayed in social media feeds.

Echo Chamber: An environment where a person only encounters information or opinions that reflect and reinforce their own.

Fact-Checking: The act of checking factual assertions in non-fictional text to determine the veracity and correctness of the factual statements.

Conclusion of Appendix

The appendix of "A Study of ClickBait" serves as a comprehensive resource, designed to extend and enrich the reader's journey through the multifaceted world of digital content. From detailed case studies to an extensive list of additional resources, this appendix has been carefully curated to provide deeper insights, further learning opportunities, and practical tools.

It is our hope that these additional materials will not only complement the main content of the book but also encourage readers to continue exploring the ever-evolving landscape of digital media. Whether it's through enhancing personal media literacy, engaging in informed discussions, or utilizing the tools and platforms provided, there is a wealth of opportunity for continued growth and understanding.

As the digital world continues to change and challenge our perceptions, the need for ongoing education, critical thinking, and ethical engagement remains paramount. This appendix is just one step in that ongoing journey, a stepping stone towards a more informed, discerning, and responsible digital world.

We invite you, the reader, to use these resources as a guide as you navigate the complexities of digital content and clickbait, and to continue to seek out knowledge and understanding in this vital and dynamic field.